Ketogenic Diet

How to Lose Weight Without Starving Yourself, Even If You're a Complete Beginner: 40+ Simple Low-Carb Recipes and Meal Plan Included

Zilker Press

Copyright © 2020 by Zilker Press

ALL RIGHTS RESERVED

No part of this book may be reproduced, stored in a retrieval system, or transmitted in any form or by any means, electronic, mechanical, photocopying, recording, scanning, or otherwise, without the prior written permission of the publisher.

Limit of Liability/Disclaimer of Warranty: the publisher and the author make no representations or warranties with respect to the accuracy or completeness of the contents of this work and specifically disclaim all warranties, including without limitation warranties of fitness for a particular purpose. No warranty may be created or extended by sales or promotional materials. The advice and strategies contained herein may not be suitable for every situation. This work is sold with the understanding that the publisher is not engaged in rendering medical, legal or other professional advice or services. If professional assistance is required, the services of a competent professional person should be sought. Neither the publisher nor the author shall be liable for damages arising herefrom. The fact that an individual, organization or website is referred to in this work as a citation and/or potential source of further information does not mean that the author or the publisher endorses the information the individuals, organization or website may provide or recommendations they/it may make. Further, readers should be aware that websites listed on this work may have changed or disappeared between when this work was written and when it is read.

ISBN: 978-1-951791-42-1

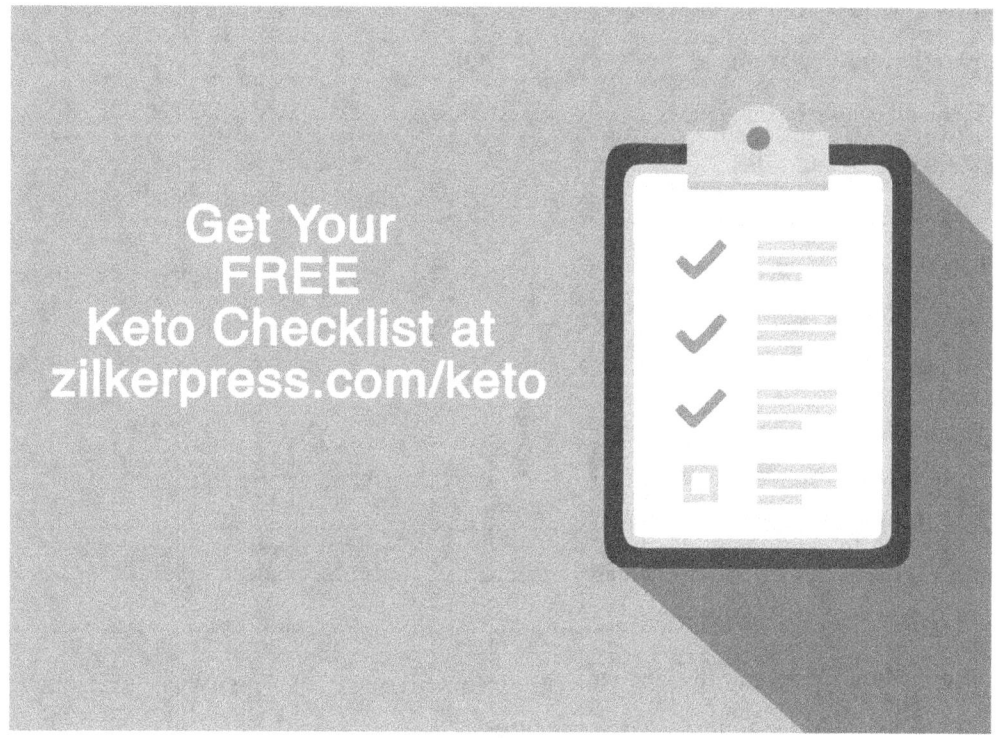

Contents

Part One: The Ketogenic Diet Explained 1
    Introduction 1
    Chapter One: Defining the Ketogenic Diet 4
    Chapter Two: History of the Ketogenic Diet 6
    Chapter Three: Variations of the Ketogenic Diet 7
        The Standard Ketogenic Diet 7
        Targeted Ketogenic Diets 8
        Cyclical Ketogenic Diets 9
        High-Protein Ketogenic Diets 10
        Paleo Keto Diet 10
        Carnivore Keto Diet 10
        Lazy Keto Diet 11
        Keto Diet for Insulin Sensitivity 12
    Chapter Four: Why Carbs Are Bad 13
    Chapter Five: Why Our Bodies Need Fats 16
    Chapter Six: Why We Need Protein 19
    Chapter Seven: Understanding Fiber 21
    Chapter Eight: Understanding Micronutrition 24
        Macronutrients vs. Micronutrients 24
        Why You Should Measure Your Micronutrient Intake 25
        Common Micronutrient Deficiencies on the Keto Diet 25
        Sodium 25
        Potassium 27
        Magnesium 28

- Calcium 29
- B Vitamins 30
- Omega-3 Fatty Acids 32
- Iodine 33
- Iron 34
- Phosphorous 35
- Vitamin A 35
- Vitamin C 35
- Vitamin K 35
- Zinc 36
- Trying to Find Foods with Micronutrients vs. Supplements 36
- When to Start Taking Supplements 37
- How Micronutrients Will Be Key to Your Keto Journey Success 37

Chapter Nine: Calculating Your Macros for the First Time 39
- Calculate Your Basal Metabolic Rate 40
- Calculate Your Total Daily Energy Expenditure 40
- Familiarize Yourself with Your Body Type 41
- Calculating Your Carbohydrate Intake 41
- Calculating Your Protein Intake 42
- Calculating Your Fat Intake 42

Chapter Ten: Keto and Its Influence on Your Overall Health 44

Chapter Eleven: The Keto Flu 45
- Common Symptoms of the Keto Flu 45
- More Tips for the Keto Flu 46

Chapter Twelve: Keto and Fasting 49
- Intermittent Fasting and Overeaters 50
- Fasting and Willpower 50

Chapter Thirteen: Keto in the Grocery Store and in the Kitchen 51

    Keto in the Grocery Store 52

    Keto in the Kitchen 55

Chapter Fourteen: What is Diabetes and How Can Keto Help? 57

    How You Can Tell You Have Type 2 Diabetes 57

    Causes of Type 2 Diabetes 58

    Risk Factors for Type 2 Diabetes 59

    Ways to Manage Type 2 Diabetes 61

    How the Keto Diet Can Help 61

    Frequently Asked Questions 61

Part Two: The 7-Day Meal Plan 74

Part Three: The Recipes 78

Breakfast & Smoothies 78

    Almond Crusted Bagels 79

    Blackberry Cheesecake Smoothie 80

    Breakfast Stuffed Bell Peppers 81

    Green Chili Quiche 82

    Ham & Asparagus Frittata 83

    Raspberry Cinnamon Smoothie 84

    Sausage Hand Pies 85

    Spinach Baked Eggs 86

Appetizers & Snacks 87

    Basil & Cheese Crackers 88

    Barbecued Almonds 89

    Cajun Portobello Chips 90

    Hot Cauliflower Bites 91

    Mushrooms Stuffed with Bacon & Cheese 92

Onion Cheese Dip	93
Spicy Glazed Pecans	94
Zucchini Pizza Bites	95

Meats & Poultry 96

Bacon & Beer Braised Cabbage	97
Beef & Blue Cheese Casserole	98
Beef Brisket with Carrots & Onions	99
Beef with Basil Sauce	101
Broccoli & Cheese Stuffed Chicken	103
Cheesesteak Wraps	104
Chicken, Cheese & Mushroom Casserole	105
Chili Verde	106
Mustard Crusted Pork Chops	108
Southern Spicy Chicken	109
Tex Mex Stir Fry	110
Turkey Cutlets with Dijon Sauce	111

Seafood & Fish 113

Cajun Salmon	114
Crab Mac 'N' Cheese	115
Creamy Clam Chowder	116
Ginger Lime Glazed Salmon	117
Parmesan Cod Nuggets	118
Salmon & Spinach Skillet	119
Shrimp Scampi	120
Steamed Spanish Clams	121

Veggies & Sides 122

Bacon & Goat Cheese Brussel Sprouts	123

Basic Cauliflower Rice 124

Cheesy Cauliflower Mash 125

Creamy Baked Squash 126

Fried Green Beans 127

Asparagus and Salmon 128

Mushroom & Spinach Cauliflower Rice 129

Roasted Italian Broccoli 130

Part One: The Ketogenic Diet Explained

Introduction

You've probably heard about the keto diet in newspapers and online articles. It's extremely popular right now, but keto diets are no new fad. In fact, they actually stem from hundreds of low-carb diets that have existed over the years.

The keto diet changes what your body uses for energy. Your body can run on two different fuels - sugar and fat. Sugar is the fuel that your body gets from carbohydrates like bread, pasta, rice, and potatoes. Fat, on the other hand, comes from eating proteins and lipids.

The keto diet is a very low-carb diet. So low, in fact, that your body has to switch to using fat for fuel from sources like eggs, avocados, butter, nuts, olive oil, and meat.

When your body runs out of sugar for fuel, it begins to convert the fat that you eat, or the fat in your body, into ketones that it burns for energy.

A diet that produces ketones as a result of what we eat is referred to as a ketogenic diet. When your body is in a state that it uses fat for fuel, it enters *ketosis*. This has several benefits.

One of these benefits for many people is weight loss. Your body becomes a fat-burning machine even when you're sleeping.

You also can have improved energy levels if you maintain your ketogenic diet properly.

The ketogenic diet is not a new concept. It stems from many other diets that are strictly low-carb and gluten-free. It's also similar to the Paleo and Atkins diets.

In fact, the Atkins diet is actually one form of the ketogenic diet. To maintain a ketogenic diet is relatively simple. All you have to do is limit your consumption of carbohydrates, which are found sugars, fruits, grain products, and other processed foods.

That means cutting out things like pizza, soda, doughnuts, bread, french fries, pasta, rice, and candy.

If you learn to adjust your eating habits and maintain your keto diet regularly, you will actually find yourself supercharged with energy. The better you adhere to the diet, the more benefits you will reap.

Modern science demonstrates that keto diets work for weight loss when followed correctly. Most people can lose their excess weight without feeling hungry.

Dieters also discover that it helps them overcome a variety of ailments like diabetes and epilepsy.

However, the keto diet is not just a quick fix for weight loss. Many people choose to stick with the ketogenic diet and make it a part of their lifestyle long after they have reached their target weight. This diet can contribute to their long-term health and well-being and help them stay fit all year-round.

Many people find the diet gives them more stable energy and blood sugar levels. Furthermore, they enjoy the clarity of mind that living on a keto diet gives them. Over time, feelings of hunger and cravings for sugar will altogether disappear.

The keto diet also makes you less likely to crave snacks. The stable energy levels associated with the ketogenic state allow you to go longer in between meals, freeing you to spend your time doing things other than thinking about eating.

Many people report that they are so satisfied with the keto diet that even if they eat all they desire, they still lose weight.

Many of them don't even need to greatly increase their exercise level in order to see results. Although exercise is good for optimal health and well-being, people on the keto diet can lose weight without implementing an exercise regimen.

In order to be successful on a keto diet, you need to learn what to eat and what not to eat. You also need to consider when you are eating.

In this book, you will learn all you need to know to get started. You will also find out about common problems people experience when they begin a keto diet and how to avoid these issues.

Additionally, you will learn how to recognize when your body is in a ketogenic state and how to get there if you are failing.

We will also discuss how to lose weight on keto, when you might expect to see weight loss, and what you can do if it feels like your weight loss has plateaued.

Finally, you will learn the common mistakes people make when they are designing ketogenic meals and how you can avoid these errors and find success more quickly.

Chapter One: Defining the Ketogenic Diet

"Ketogenic" is a low-carb diet that allows you to choose protein and fat for your calorie source over carbohydrates.

To obtain a ketogenic state, you must cut back on your intake of sugar, bread, pastries, rice, and more. In order to enter a ketogenic state, you need to consume less than 50g[1] of carbohydrates a day. That means if you are consuming a 2,000-calorie-a-day diet, it's only 5 to 10 percent of your daily nutritional intake. The other macronutrients you intake are 70 to 80 percent fat and about 20 to 25 percent protein.

The amount of protein you eat can be calculated based on your ideal weight. In general, it should be at least 0.75g per pound of your target weight.[2]

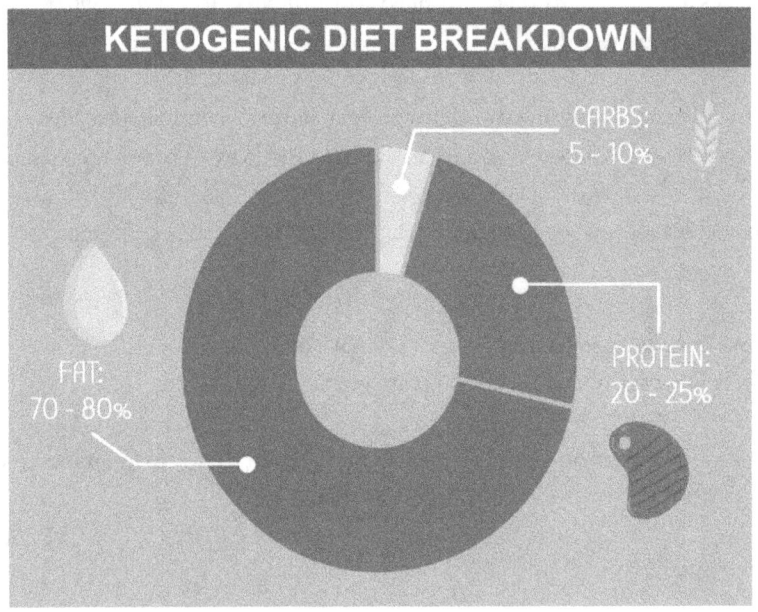

---

[1] Masood W, Uppaluri KR. Ketogenic Diet. [Updated 2019 Mar 21]. In: StatPearls [Internet]. Treasure Island (FL): StatPearls Publishing; 2019 Jan-. Available from: https://www.ncbi.nlm.nih.gov/books/NBK499830/
[2] Bonjour JP. Dietary protein: an essential nutrient for bone health. J Am Coll Nutr. 2005;24(6 Suppl):526S-36S.

When your daily carb intake is less than 50g, your body will run out of fuel and begin to switch from running on blood sugar to running on fat. This change usually takes about two days to complete. This does not account for the keto flu which can take longer to adjust to. During your transition to the keto diet, it's common to feel flu-like symptoms and be lethargic.

These symptoms can last for one to two weeks depending on your body. This is because your liver and muscle glycogen should empty after about sixteen hours. But, if you continue to consume the residual carbs in vegetables, it can be a more drawn-out process.

You may also notice that your energy levels drop. If you continue with the diet, however, you will notice your energy levels return to normal—they may even improve. This is a simple adaptation phase and is a sign that your body has officially entered the ketogenic state. Although some people observe the ketogenic diet as part of their lifestyle to help them manage their weight and health conditions, many people use it as a short-term diet meant to help them drop weight quickly.

Many practitioners of the keto diet see their weight loss drop off after a few months on the diet. If they ever choose to switch back to a "Standard American Diet" (S.A.D. for short), they will undoubtedly regain water weight and possibly some fat if they transition poorly.

In order to be successful in losing and keeping off weight using the keto diet, you need to make informed decisions about your meals on a long-term basis. Maintaining a keto diet should be seen as a lifestyle change, not a short-term fix.

Chapter Two: History of the Ketogenic Diet

The ketogenic diet was first used as therapy in 1921 by Russel Wilder as a way to treat epilepsy. Wilder was the first to coin the term "ketogenic diet."

The diet has been around for longer than that under other names and is actually considered to be a very natural diet for humans. Hunter and gatherer civilizations would often eat diets consisting of meat and vegetables.

After its initial success as a diet for epilepsy patients, it became a regular option for a therapeutic diet for pediatric patients suffering from epilepsy. It was used widely for years with continued positive results.

When anti-epileptic agents and medications were invented several years later, the diet began to lose popularity. People found that it was easier to take medication to deal with their condition rather than to restructure their body's entire metabolic system to run on different fuel.

But, the ketogenic diet reemerged several years later as a means to lose weight. It has now gained a lot of attention in the media and has become a proven weight loss solution for many dieters.

Chapter Three: Variations of the Ketogenic Diet

The simpler a diet is, the easier it is for people to follow. Why's that? Because it leaves no guesswork as to what is and what isn't off-limits. We, as humans, are creatures of habit. While we like change from time to time, having a solid understanding of what we know to be effective is what leads to success in the long run. Fortunately, the ketogenic diet is a very simple diet to follow!

It's very easy to keep up with, and coming up with creative dishes for the meals is also not difficult since there are so many options. Trying to change up your old-school favorites to keep in-line with your keto diet is more a matter of adaptation than restriction.

For those who are obsessed with avocado, butter, bacon, and cream, the diet can be very easy to adjust to. But, those who are used to a lot of processed foods and added sugars are advised to be patient in the beginning. It will take time for their body and mind to adjust to their new lifestyle.

So then, how did this diet become so popular? Well, in actuality, many people are already on some popular variation of the ketogenic diet. These variations make the diet more appealing to long-term users.

The Standard Ketogenic Diet

The standard ketogenic diet focuses all meals around meat, vegetables, and fat. In order to get enough fat on a standard keto diet, you'll probably eat more than 100 grams of fat every day.

This is the same amount that you would find in ¾ of a cup of butter. For many people, that's about three times the amount that they're currently eating.

While you're upping your fat intake, you also need to cut your carbohydrate intake from more than 300g per day (which is standard) to less than 50g.

This is about the number of carbohydrates that you would find in a blueberry muffin. To provide a wholesome nutritious balance to your meals add leafy greens and vegetables that don't contain too much starch.

Initially, you may not want to eat fruit often because of fructose; the sugar found in fruit can pull your body out of a ketogenic state if you consume too much of it.

You'll also need to eat at least 0.63g/lb of your ideal body weight in protein each day in the form of about four ounces of meat, fish, or poultry.[3]

For a 130-lb man or woman, this amounts to 82.68g/day.

If you don't eat enough protein, you risk losing bone density in addition to weight. By eating the right amount of protein, you preserve your bone density while still losing weight.

Targeted Ketogenic Diets

Targeted ketogenic diets are more popular with people who are highly active, like athletes. Those who need to refill their muscle glycogen are allowed to eat an extra 20 to 30 grams of carbohydrates or add protein (0.3g protein per kg body weight post-exercise) right after they finish a workout.

This is done so that your body has more fuel for the recovery process. While this amount is very moderate, it can make a major difference in the way an athlete's body performs. Targeted ketogenic diets are designed for people who enjoy the way they feel when observing the keto lifestyle, but who find their bodies need more carbohydrates to function at sustained high-energy levels for an extended period of time.[4]

On a targeted keto diet, you will still see weight loss, but these targeted (supplemental) carbs will help muscle development.

---

[3] Shams-white MM, Chung M, Du M, et al. Dietary protein and bone health: a systematic review and meta-analysis from the National Osteoporosis Foundation. Am J Clin Nutr. 2017;105(6):1528-1543.

[4] Koopman R, Beelen M, Stellingwerff T, et al. Coingestion of carbohydrate with protein does not further augment postexercise muscle protein synthesis. Am J Physiol Endocrinol Metab. 2007;293(3):E833-42.

Your carb count for the day will still be significantly lower than a standard diet, with followers eating just 70 to 80 grams of carbs per day post-workout. Of course, since these carbs are only post-workout, these extra carbs would not be consumed on non-workout days.

The goal is to aim for carbohydrates that will fill our muscle glycogen. This means that we are going to aim for sources of glucose rather than fructose or lactose. We can find glucose-rich carbs in starchy foods like white rice and potatoes. One cup of either option will give you all the extra glucose you will need post-workout.

The reason why we avoid carbohydrates with fructose and lactose (coming from fruit and dairy products) is because these sugars help to refill our liver glycogen rather than our muscle glycogen. Due to this, they are less effective for muscle building and should be avoided post-workout.

With all of that being said, a meal very rich in protein post-workout is theorized to be equally as effective as the targeted carbs. This is because the excess protein that your muscles don't use will go through gluconeogenesis and will fill your muscle glycogen that way.

Cyclical Ketogenic Diets

The cyclical ketogenic diet (often abbreviated CKD), like the Targeted Ketogenic Diet, involves cycling starchy carbs in and out of your diet in order to maximize muscle growth by topping off your muscle glycogen stores. Doing this will pull you in and out of ketosis, forcing you to be more metabolically flexible. Of course, the carbs that are being cycled in or out are whole foods—they are not processed sugar or wheat products.

This is only recommended to those with at least four to six months of experience on the ketogenic diet. For most practitioners, a keto cycle will include five to six days of dieting using ketogenic restrictions, followed by one to two non-keto days, usually on the weekend.

Some cyclers also choose to save up their non-keto days for special occasions like holidays or outings with friends. While keto cycling can still be a great way to achieve weight loss, you should try to stick to wholesome and unprocessed foods on your days off. Otherwise, you may see your weight loss begin to yo-yo or plateau.

That means eating carefully selected foods like fruits, starchy veggies, and whole grains on your days off, rather than filling your table with highly-processed foods and refined sugar.

Keto cycling isn't for everyone. It can be difficult for your body and metabolism to constantly be in a state of flux. If you find yourself having consistently low-energy levels or stalling with your weight loss, you may want to consider another variation of the keto diet or return to a standard diet.

High-Protein Ketogenic Diets

Another common variation of the ketogenic diet is a high-protein option. Under this version of the diet, you would eat approximately 120g of protein per day. That's the equivalent of eating about four– 4-oz. servings of meat or fish.

At the same time, your diet is still restricted to less than 10 percent of your calories coming from carbohydrates. This means that another 130g of fat should be consumed every day in order to reach a healthy calorie count.

Many people find this version of the keto diet to be much easier to follow. This is because many Americans are not used to eating such a large percentage of fat every day.

But, high-protein ketogenic diets work well for many people. The protein process (gluconeogenesis) puts your body in a demand-driven state. If your body doesn't use the proteins that are available, they won't be stored for later.

Paleo Keto Diet

A paleo keto diet combines the paleo diet, emulating foods of our ancestors, and the keto diet, which is low in carbohydrates.

It focuses on consuming natural and nutritious foods with large amounts of energy deriving from animal sources. If you find yourself on a paleo keto diet, you might eat a lot of steak and fresh produce.

Carnivore Keto Diet

Carnivore keto (also referred to as the "Ultimate Elimination Diet") is similar to the ancestral Paleo concept of dieting in the sense that we only eat foods that were available to us thousands of years ago.

A carnivore diet revolves around eating ruminant animal red meat (cattle, lamb, goat, antelope, elk, or deer). Thus, a single day's intake of food might consist of 2lbs+ of just red meat, divided into two sittings. Non-ruminants (pork, chicken, duck, and fish) are considered secondary, along with organ meats and eggs. The fat that is used is naturally occurring fat from the animal (i.e., tallow [from a cow] and lard [from a pig]).

The carnivore diet is the "animal produce diet," which includes meat, fish, poultry, eggs, and dairy. Most carnivores don't eat three times a day because they are eating the most nutrient-dense food on the planet. This is the most ancestral way of eating.

Homo sapiens have lived for millions of years, thriving on red meat and the land. It is only in the past fifty years that we have had access to every food on the planet in one grocery store.

The carnivore diet helps with mental clarity, digestion, inflammation, weight loss, autoimmune disease, and many other metabolic conditions. This diet looks into connecting the human with the earth by only consuming products from whole regional animals, engaging in a zero-waste protocol. While newly popular, this diet has seen quite a lot of success from those who have tried it.

The adaptation period of this diet can sometimes cause diarrhea, but this can be regulated by buying a lipase enzyme supplement to help with digesting the extra fat. Once the body adapts to the extra fat being consumed, the transition period will be over and it should be smooth sailing. This transition period usually doesn't last for more than two weeks. Sometimes—if the individual slowly eases into the carnivore diet—it doesn't even happen.

Lazy Keto Diet

The most important part of the diet is that you stick to eating low-carb foods and emphasize your fat intake.

To maintain a ketogenic state, you should eat just 5 percent of your calories from carbohydrates each day. For most people, that's about 20 to 30 grams.

In everyday life, however, most people don't walk around with culinary measuring tools that serve accurate portions.

On a lazy keto diet, as long as you hit that number, you don't have to pay close attention to the percentage of fat versus protein that you eat.

The lazy keto diet may seem tempting to you, but it can also cause a lot of problems. You may find yourself hungrier on this form of diet if you don't eat enough fat.

You also might not focus on the quality of the nutrients that you are eating. You may miss out on fats with important vitamins and minerals. It is also easy to consume too few calories in a day if you don't pay attention to your fat intake. This can make you tired and lethargic and more likely to break your diet.

Keto Diet for Insulin Sensitivity

For those who are using the keto diet to adjust their insulin sensitivity levels, you may find benefits by adjusting your diet to just 50g of carbohydrates per day.

At this level, you won't feel the same complete energy shift that occurs on a fully ketogenic diet. But, you may find your insulin levels to be more stable.

Chapter Four: Why Carbs Are Bad

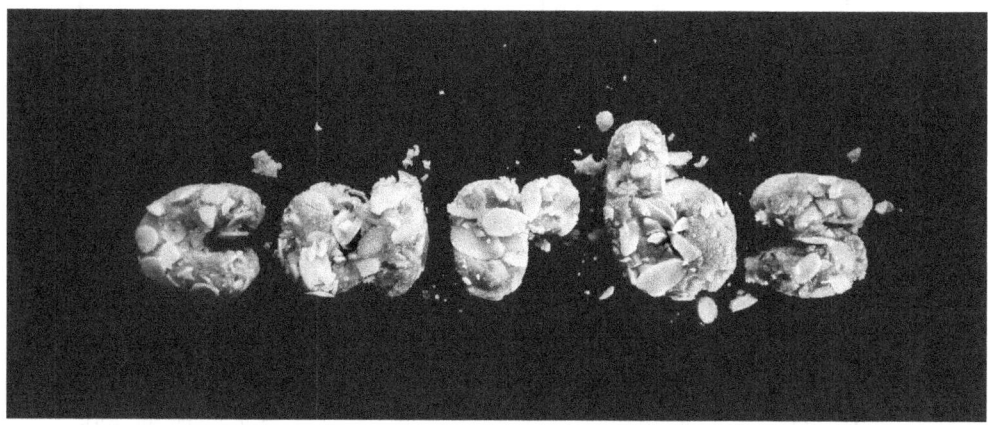

It is completely possible to be healthy with some carb consumption. A lot of individuals, however, have eaten enough carbs to last them a lifetime. Never before has the modern world been exposed to such an excess of breads, desserts, and processed foods. Sadly, this has had a negative effect on our society and its peoples' general well-being. This means that for most people, trying out the keto diet and eliminating this excess of carbs can do their body a world of good.

When carbohydrates are consumed in excess, we start to become insulin resistant. This means that we have consumed so many carbohydrates that the hormone that's in charge of handling all of these carbs basically says, "I quit, I can't do this anymore." This hormone is called insulin. When your insulin is inoperable you can find yourself with diabetes, heart disease, neurological (brain) diseases, cancer, and hypertension.

We, as a society, have been conditioned to reach for potato chips and other easy snack foods when hungry. This will put anyone on the fast-track to insulin resistance and the diseases that come with it.[5]

---

[5] Jung CH, Choi KM. Impact of High-Carbohydrate Diet on Metabolic Parameters in Patients with Type 2 Diabetes. Nutrients. 2017;9(4)

There are two different kinds of refined carbohydrates - sugars and refined grains. These dietary sources have been stripped of much of their natural nutrients including fiber, vitamins, and minerals. This is why many people refer to them as "empty" calories.

Let's take a closer look at how eating large amounts of refined carbohydrates can impact your body's performance.

1. They Have a High Glycemic Index

The problem with refined carbohydrates is that they are digested quickly and have a high glycemic index. This means they can cause your blood sugar and insulin levels to quickly spike after meals. This effect has been shown to lead to increased incidences of overeating and higher rates of disease.[6]

When you eat a meal that is rich in carbohydrates, you may feel full and satisfied initially, but this feeling doesn't last. This is why sometimes after having a carb-rich meal or snack you'll be hungry just three hours later. On the other hand, when you eat foods that are lower on the glycemic index, you'll feel full for six hours. This is why those on the keto diet often start fasting. When you choose to cut out the carbs, you aren't as hungry anymore, and fasting just sort of happens. That being said, if you don't feel like fasting, then your body probably isn't ready to do it yet. Keep eating. Eventually your body will get all the nutrition it needs. At this point, you will realize that you're not hungry and that you can skip a meal.[7]

2. Carbohydrates Increase Your Risk of Developing Heart Disease and Type 2 Diabetes

Heart disease is one of the most deadly killers on the planet. The famous Dr. Kraft once observed that those with cardiovascular disease simply have undiagnosed diabetes. That being said, those who suffer from heart disease or who have a family history of it should check with their doctor to see how well their insulin is working. It is also recommended that these individuals consider adopting the keto diet to lower their risk of heart disease and type 2 diabetes. Yes, these two conditions are related. Having problems with insulin has been shown to damage the endothelium, which in turn can lead to heart

---

[6] Gomes, Júnia Maria Geraldo, Fabrini, Sabrina Pinheiro, & Alfenas, Rita de Cássia Gonçalves. (2017). Low glycemic index diet reduces body fat and attenuates inflammatory and metabolic responses in patients with type 2 diabetes. *Archives of Endocrinology and Metabolism, 61*(2), 137-144. Epub September 05, 2016.https://dx.doi.org/10.1590/2359-3997000000206

[7] Belinda Lennerz, Jochen K Lennerz, Food Addiction, High-Glycemic-Index Carbohydrates, and Obesity, Clinical Chemistry, Volume 64, Issue 1, 1 January 2018, Pages 64–71

disease. The diabetes epidemic is an incredibly common illness that affects hundreds of millions of people around the world.[8]

Now that you know how type 2 diabetes and heart disease are related, you can understand how important it is to be aware of your insulin resistance. Remaining vigilant on this matter may help you avoid such health complications.

---

[8] Zuñiga YL, Rebello SA, Oi PL, et al. Rice and noodle consumption is associated with insulin resistance and hyperglycemia in an Asian population. Br J Nutr. 2014;111(6):1118-28.

Chapter Five: Why Our Bodies Need Fats

According to the American Heart Association, fats are an important part of a healthy diet.[9] Fats, also known as lipids, play an essential role in supporting cell growth as well as manufacturing energy for your body.

Fats act as cushion for your organs and are used to help keep your body warm in cold environments. They also help keep you satiated. But that's not all.

---

[9] "Dietary Fats." Heart.org, American Heart Association, 23 Mar. 2014, www.heart.org/en/healthy-living/healthy-eating/eat-smart/fats/dietary-fats.

Fats also are used to absorb nutrients that your body couldn't otherwise process and they are used in the production process for hormones. Without fats, you simply wouldn't grow and develop properly. They supply you with a sustainable energy source and help you regulate your vitamin intake.

On a keto diet, it's important to pick the right types of fat to eat. After all, they will be your primary source of energy.

In general, there are four different kinds of fats:

1. Saturated fats (think of solid fats at room temperature, like butter)
2. Trans fats (which have been eradicated from the US diet market)
3. Monounsaturated fats
4. Polyunsaturated fats (think of liquid fats at room temperature, like oil)

Each of these types of fats have different chemical structures, as well as differing physical properties that make them better or worse for your body during digestion.

A Note on Saturated Fats

Saturated fats are naturally occurring in breast milk, meat, and eggs. At one time they were considered to be bad for your heart. Now, however, newly published studies call into question that finding.

Saturated fats can be a healthy part of a keto diet and are no longer believed to increase your risk of developing heart disease. In fact, they may even help to optimize your cholesterol levels and boost your cellular integrity.

Calories in Fat

Regardless of what kind of fat you consume, you will absorb 9 calories for every gram of fat you eat. This measurement makes fat much more energy-dense than other macronutrients like carbohydrates and proteins that have just 4 calories per gram.

A Note on Getting Used to Eating More Fat

At first, eating a lot of fat may feel out of the ordinary and, let's be honest, overly tasty. Try to think of as many diverse ways to try new fats as possible during your first few weeks on the diet.

With this approach, you'll experience the beauty of this diet early on. Familiarize yourself with new ingredients, or just add a lot of butter to your diet. Butter, as you may already know, can add a lot of flavor to your food and make the cooking process more exciting.

Types of Fat to Eat on Keto

As a general rule, if the fat you are eating is naturally occurring in your food, then it's a keto-friendly item and you should eat it. However, if an item is processed with refined vegetable oils, it's best to avoid it. Choose an unrefined source of fat instead.

If you're looking for healthy sources of fats, consider:
- Fatty beef cuts
- Fatty pork cuts
- Dark chicken meat
- Poultry skin
- Eggs
- Coconut oil
- Cocoa butter
- Lard

Chapter Six: Why We Need Protein

Protein is a very important component for most of the cells in your body. In fact, both your nails and the hair on your body are made almost entirely of proteins.

It's also used as a building block for the tissues that make up your flesh, muscles, and bone. Proteins are found in your body's enzymes, your hormones, and other important chemicals.

Protein is one of the three primary macronutrients of the body—the other two being carbohydrates and fat.

This means that your body generally requires large amounts of protein. Your body also needs several vitamins and minerals, referred to as micronutrients. These substances will be discussed shortly.

Unlike the other two macronutrients, proteins cannot be stored in the body. This means that whenever your body needs a fresh supply of protein, you must consume food to provide it.

How Much Protein?

Protein is one of the most essential macronutrients in your entire body. On average, the American population does not consume enough protein to support their body on a daily basis.

A great rule of thumb is 1g of animal-based protein for every pound of your targeted body weight.

The reason why it's important for protein to come from animal sources is that proteins are made up of twenty amino acids—nine of which are completely essential and need to be eaten for us to obtain them. There are zero plant foods that have all nine essential amino acids. On the other hand, any animal product will automatically have every single one.

This recommended amount of protein applies to everyone. Athletes, however, might choose to consume more protein to support the extra effort that they exert during physical activities. So yes, even sedentary people need 1g of animal protein per pound of their goal weight.

One of the most nutrient-rich foods you can have for dinner is a steak. Eating red meat is extremely compatible with the human body's natural physiology and biochemistry. Other great sources of protein come from cows, pigs, fish, poultry, and eggs. Dairy can also be consumed, but that depends on your dairy tolerance levels.

How to Choose a Great Protein

Not all proteins are created equal. In fact, we have as many processed meats as we do processed carbs. Try to aim for the meats that come from behind the meat counter and avoid those that are filled with additives.

It also helps that (on the keto diet) you will be separating these meats from their carbohydrate-rich counterpart - bread. When you take out carbohydrates, you actually reduce the risk factors associated with these processed meats.

But, as a general rule, you should opt for healthier protein sources like steak, fish, and chicken. With fish, you are able to consume heart-healthy omega-3 fatty acids and other nutrients that are good for you. Fish is also an excellent source of fat for the keto diet if you choose a high-fat option like salmon.

Poultry is another great option because it is low in calories. While you may be tempted to remove the skin, leaving it on is a great way to up your fat intake for the day if you're lacking calories.

But the ultimate choice for many people on the keto diet is steak, which has a great vitamin B complex, choline, creatine, heme iron, and a great Omega 3-6 ratio. It comes with a healthy serving of naturally occurring fat to keep you healthy and satisfied.

Chapter Seven: Understanding Fiber

If you watch television at all, you've probably seen at least one commercial that encourages you to eat more fiber. But, have you ever given much thought as to why people say it's so good for your health?

Eating the right amount of fiber (mostly found in low-carb vegetables such as lettuce, broccoli, cauliflower, zucchini, etc.) is known to prevent constipation.

But it also offers other health benefits. For example, it can help you to stabilize your weight and lower your risk of diseases like diabetes, heart disease, and several forms of cancer.

People also like fiber because the body doesn't digest it and, therefore, it can't contribute to weight gain. Let's take a closer look at what fiber is and the role it plays in the body.

Soluble vs. Insoluble Fiber

Dietary fiber is the part of food that is known as roughage or bulk. Unlike macronutrients (fats, proteins, carbs), it can't be absorbed or digested by the body. Possessing intestinal cleansing properties, fiber simply passes through your stomach and out of your body. Contrary to popular belief, a diet very high in fiber can cause problems with digestion. Try experimenting with higher-fiber weeks and lower-fiber weeks to see how you need to adjust your optimal fiber intake.

There are two different kinds of fiber - soluble and insoluble. All plants contain a mixture of the two, but some will have more soluble fiber while others will have more insoluble fiber.

Soluble fiber dissolves in water, making a gel-like substance (think of oatmeal that's been soaked or heated in water). This substance can be used by the body to lower your glycemic index so that it can slow down digestion, leaving you fuller for longer. Sometimes though, having too much can lead to bloating and constipation, so having lots of soluble fiber sometimes isn't ideal. The only four examples of soluble fibers on the keto diet are:
- Avocados
- Brussels sprouts
- Broccoli
- Nuts

The reason why there are only four is because most soluble fiber options come from carbohydrates and don't really have their place in the keto diet. It is entirely possible to survive without soluble fibers in your diet. We recommend trying to do two weeks with soluble fibers. If you notice no difference in digestion that means that your body can easily digest them. If you do experience any discomfort once these have been incorporated into your diet, you'll know that soluble fibers don't agree with you and that you should not be having them.

Insoluble fiber, on the other hand, does not dissolve in water and cannot be digested. Most insoluble fibers are found on the skin of fruits and vegetables. This explains why corn comes out of you exactly the same way it goes in. It's because your body does not have the ability to break it down and digest it. As with the soluble fiber, test to see how much fiber you can tolerate in your diet to see what works best for you. Sources of insoluble fibers include:
- Cauliflower
- Zucchini
- Celery
- Green beans
- Other leafy green vegetables

Please note that if your gut has healing to do, then you might do well on a lower-fiber diet or on a higher-fiber diet. It is up to you to see what your body tolerates and what you feel best consuming.

Fiber cannot be destroyed by cooking, but you can modify fiber content by peeling your vegetables and by taking their seeds out. You can also lower your fiber by replacing your vegetables with animal products. Know that it is completely acceptable to have a zero-fiber (meaning no plants, and only animal products) meal on the keto diet.

Fiber and the Keto Diet

Overall, a keto diet consists mainly of eating meat and veggies cooked in fat.

This means you should have no problem getting the amount of fiber that's right for you. It's important to remember that all of your carbohydrates in the keto diet will be coming from plant-based foods, meaning vegetables. This is represented through your net carbs.

Net carbs, meaning the total amount of carbohydrates your body will absorb, can be found by subtracting the fiber content of a food from its total carbohydrate content. When you're on a keto diet, some people shoot for 20g of net carbs, with some people eating as much as 50 grams of net carbs a day.

Imagine you decide to eat one cup of cauliflower. The label says that it contains 5g of carbohydrates, but it also lists 2g of fiber. If you subtract the difference, you will see that only 3 of the grams will count toward your carb intake for the day.

Chapter Eight: Understanding Micronutrition

Starting a keto diet means that you will be eliminating certain foods, right? You may begin to wonder how you will be able to get enough nutrients.

You don't want to end up with a vitamin or mineral deficiency that seriously affects your health. All it takes to ensure proper nutrition on the keto diet is a little bit of planning.

Rest assured that you won't be missing out on any essential nutrients from potatoes, corn, or wheat products. The foods you eat on the keto diet will give your body all of the macronutrients it needs.

Macronutrients vs. Micronutrients

All foods contain some combination of micronutrients and macronutrients. The only macronutrients are fats, carbohydrates, and proteins.

Each of these forms of energy provides calories for your body. Protein and carbohydrates have 4 calories, while fats have 9 calories per gram. Micronutrients, on the other hand, are nutrients that are found in only very small amounts in the human body.

They are used for growth and development and include vitamins, phytochemicals, fatty acids, trace elements, minerals, and antioxidants.

Micronutrients are used both to slow down the aging process of your body and to protect it from disease. They are at work in nearly every system in your body to ensure they are running optimally.

Unlike macronutrients, micronutrients cannot provide the body with energy. For that reason, they are not measured in calories and often aren't mentioned on food labels in any meaningful way.

Why You Should Measure Your Micronutrient Intake

Most people may find themselves deficient in certain micronutrients on a daily basis, even if they're not dieting, so they take vitamins/supplements.

By eating more organic and grass-fed beef, eggs from pasture-fed chicken, and leafy greens, and including all of the essential and natural vitamins your body needs, you help to increase your brain's cognitive function and your bone density, decrease your risk of infection, and more.[10]

No matter what kind of diet you are trying, it's important that you take some time to think about how it will affect your micronutritional intake. If you design your keto diet to hit the right macro targets but all you do is fill up on butter and bacon, then you will be depriving your body of said micronutrients.

The best way to avoid developing the keto flu is to make sure you consume a regular dose of the right micronutrients. At the beginning of the diet, it may be a good idea to take some supplements.

Common Micronutrient Deficiencies on the Keto Diet

Many people who have heard about the keto diet have also heard about the flu-like symptoms that can accompany it. Most of the time, this suffering is not caused by what people on the keto diet are eating; it's a result of what they aren't eating.

Missing out on major micronutrients can cause you to feel tired, dizzy, and sick. Let's take a look at some of the most common micronutrient deficiencies for people on the keto diet so that you know what to look for when you start your meal plan.

Sodium

Surprisingly enough, the most common mineral and electrolyte deficiency that appears after starting a ketogenic diet is sodium. Sodium is a very important nutritional ingredient for the body.

While at some points in history it has been vilified in the media as a way to exacerbate cardiovascular disease, this has now been proven to be a myth.

---

[10] Shenkin, A. "Micronutrients in health and disease." *Postgraduate medical journal* vol. 82,971 (2006): 559-67. doi:10.1136/pgmj.2006.047670

In reality, sodium plays an important role in helping your body control its blood pressure, retain the right water levels, and absorb other micronutrients. When you start the ketogenic diet, you will notice that it has a diuretic effect. This means that you will be peeing often.

The reason is that once your body enters the ketosis state, it will begin to shed water and electrolytes. If you play sports, the effect will be even more profound. This is because the body excretes sodium through the sweat glands as well.

Symptoms that indicate your body may be deficient in sodium include headaches, extreme fatigue, and inability to perform strenuous activities. A great simple source for sodium is bouillon cubes or bone broth. Try to aim for at least 3 to 6 grams of sodium per day, which is about 12 grams of table salt (the equivalent of one tablespoon).[11]

---

[11] O'donnell M, Mente A, Rangarajan S, et al. Urinary sodium and potassium excretion, mortality, and cardiovascular events. N Engl J Med. 2014;371(7):612-23.

Potassium

Potassium is another electrolyte that your body can lose. When you are deficient in potassium, you may find yourself feeling constipated, irritable, or physically weak.

You may also notice that you are losing muscle mass and developing skin problems like acne. More serious conditions caused by a potassium deficiency include an irregular heart rate and, in extreme cases, heart failure.

To avoid any of these outcomes, you should aim to consume about 4,500 milligrams of potassium every day while you are on the keto diet.

Note: It is very unlikely that you will become deficient of potassium on the keto diet.

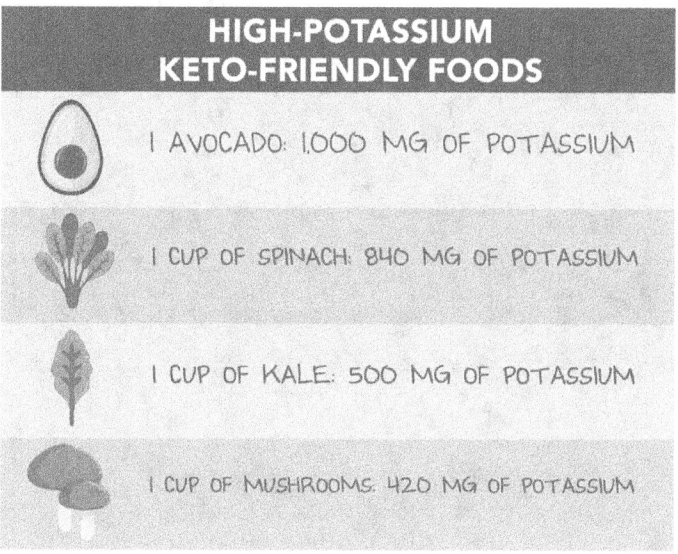

Magnesium

Magnesium is a micronutrient that is responsible for hundreds of different biochemical functions that occur every day in your body. It's both a mineral and an electrolyte that is needed for protein synthesis, energy production in the form of ATM, cell reproduction, and fatty acid formation.

If you are experiencing a deficiency in magnesium, you may find yourself feeling dizzy, tired, and crampy. In order to ensure you are getting enough magnesium while you are on a keto diet, you should consume about 500 milligrams per day.

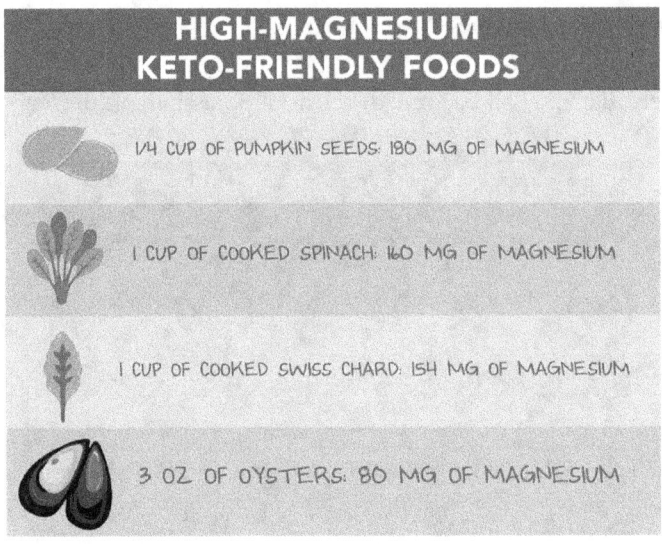

Calcium

Calcium is another extremely important micronutrient in the body. It's used to form and strengthen both our bones and our teeth. It's also a mineral and electrolyte that is used to assist in blood clotting, regulating blood pressure, and sending signals in between nerve cells.[12]

Our bodies contain large stores of calcium in both our bones and our teeth, but it's still a micronutrient we need to consume often. In order to ensure you are getting enough calcium while you're on a keto diet, you should aim for at least 1,000 to 2,000 milligrams of calcium per day.

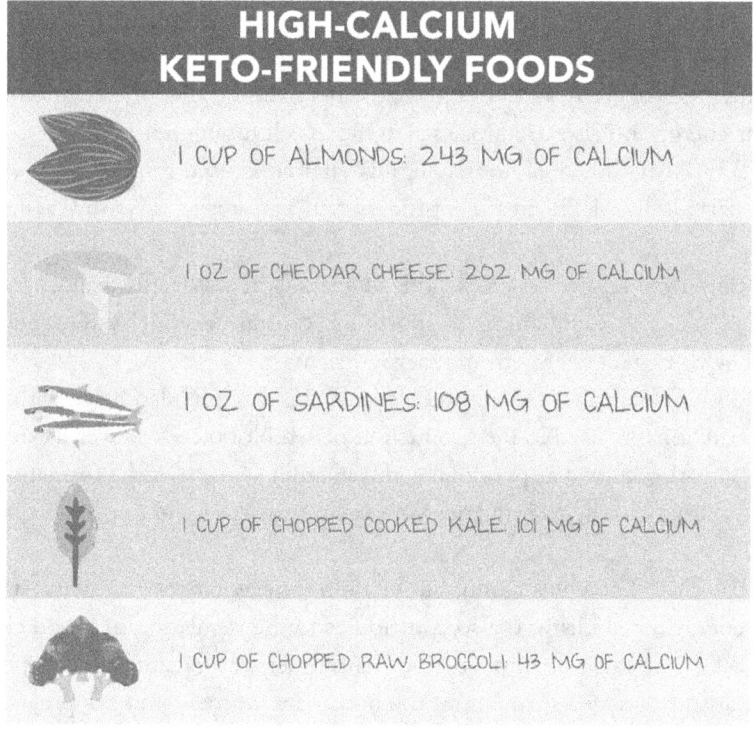

---

[12] Cao JJ, Nielsen FH. Acid diet (high-meat protein) effects on calcium metabolism and bone health. Curr Opin Clin Nutr Metab Care. 2010;13(6):698-702.

B Vitamins

There are seven major types of B vitamins, all with their own complex role to play in the body. Many people choose to take vitamin B supplements to ensure they get all of the different kinds in one pill.

Keto dieters don't actually have too much to fear when it comes to vitamin B deficiency, since most are having lots of leafy green vegetables and healthy portions of meat.

If you choose to take a vitamin B supplement, it may include:

- Vitamin B1 - Also known as thiamin, this vitamin is crucial for the breakdown of macronutrients like carbs, fats, and proteins. It's necessary for the creation of the ATP form of cellular energy and also used to assist in nerve cell functioning.
- Vitamin B2 - Also known as riboflavin, this vitamin is used to process fats and amino acids. It's also part of the ATP creation process and can act as an antioxidant in some bodily situations.
- Vitamin B3 - Also known as niacin, this vitamin is necessary for cellular respiration. It also assists with memory functioning, supports the central nervous system, helps create healthy skin, and helps extract energy from macronutrients.
- Vitamin B5 - Also known as pantothenic acid, this vitamin also helps with the extraction of ATP. In addition, it's used in the production of red blood cells as well as steroid hormones.
- Vitamin B6 - Also known as pyridoxine, this vitamin is used for the formation of proteins and red blood cells; it also helps influence your brain processes and improve your immune system function.
- Vitamin B7 - Also known as biotin, this vitamin is necessary for fat synthesis as well as amino acid and energy metabolism. It also contributes to the regulation of blood cholesterol levels.
- Vitamin B9 - Also known as folate, this vitamin helps to create red blood cells that are then used to transport oxygen throughout the body. For women who are pregnant, folate is used to assist in the development of the fetal nervous system and help with cellular growth.
- Vitamin B12 - Also known as cyanocobalamin, this vitamin is one of the most well-known of all of the B vitamins. It has very serious health benefits and can provide mental clarity as well as assist in the formation of red blood cells. It also helps to break down fatty acids, which helps your body to produce energy.

When someone is deficient in vitamin B, they may experience psychological symptoms. They could become confused, angry, paranoid, or depressed.

They could also develop heart palpitations and insomnia and have tingling in their hands and feet and trouble when they try to walk. People who are trying to ingest more B vitamins generally eat grass-fed beef, fish, and dairy products.

Fortunately, a full vitamin B complex is available through animal products.

Omega-3 Fatty Acids

Omega-3 fatty acids are used to help with several important bodily processes including:
- Inflammation reduction
- Development of the brain
- Cardiovascular health
- Oxygen transportation in the blood
- Reducing blood pressure

If you eat just a few servings of fatty fish each week, like salmon, you will be able to get enough omega-3 fatty acids in your diet naturally.

Many people who do not like to consume fish, however, prefer to get their omega-3s through supplements. In general, you should aim for about 4,000 milligrams worth of omega-3 fatty acids each week.

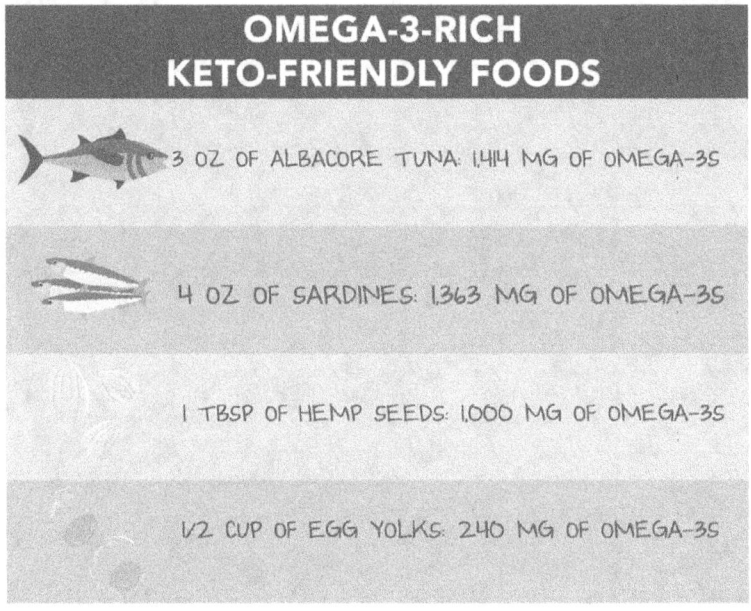

Iodine

Iodine is a vital mineral for thyroid hormone level regulation. Without proper levels, you're in danger of hypothyroidism, a condition that causes weakness, weight gain, and skin conditions.

Because iodine is such an important micronutrient and used to be harder to come by in communities that were far from the sea, it's now added to table salt. If you consume sea salt or pink Himalayan salt though, the natural levels of iodine will not be as much as you are used to.

To make up for that, you can find iodine in other natural food sources. Vegetables that come from the ocean, like kelp, are great for relieving the symptoms of hypothyroidism. In order to stay healthy, you should consume at least 150 micrograms of iodine every day.

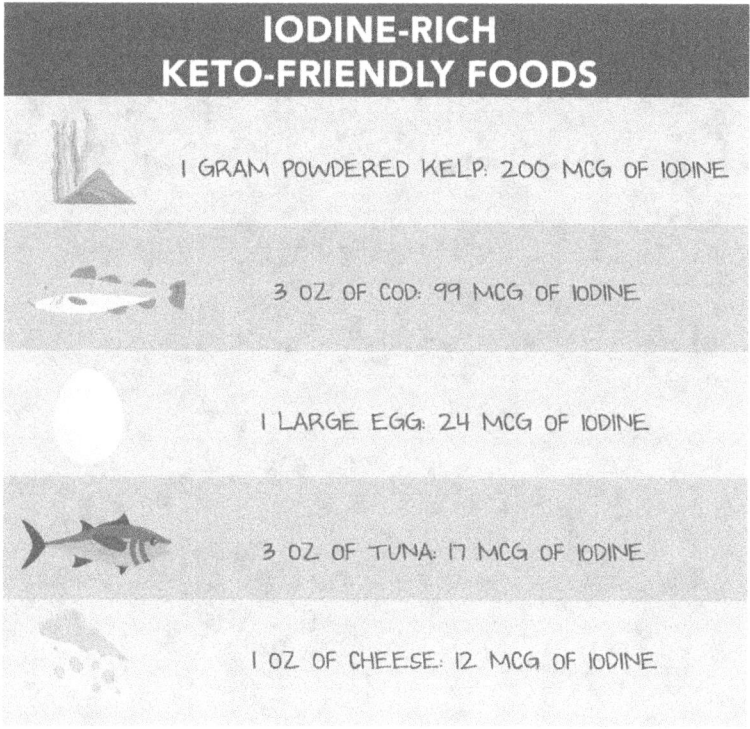

Iron

Iron is another essential nutrient for the body. It assists in the formation of hemoglobin, which is the substance necessary for transferring the oxygen in your lungs to your blood.

It's also used for improving muscle function, increasing brain function, and promoting a healthy metabolic rate.

In order to maintain a balanced diet while on keto, you should have at least 8 to 30 milligrams of heme iron every day. In order to get enough of the right form of iron in your diet, you need to either eat red meat regularly or take a heme iron supplement.

Please note that non-heme plant-based iron is practically useless to human physiology. Most, if not all, of your iron should come from animal sources.

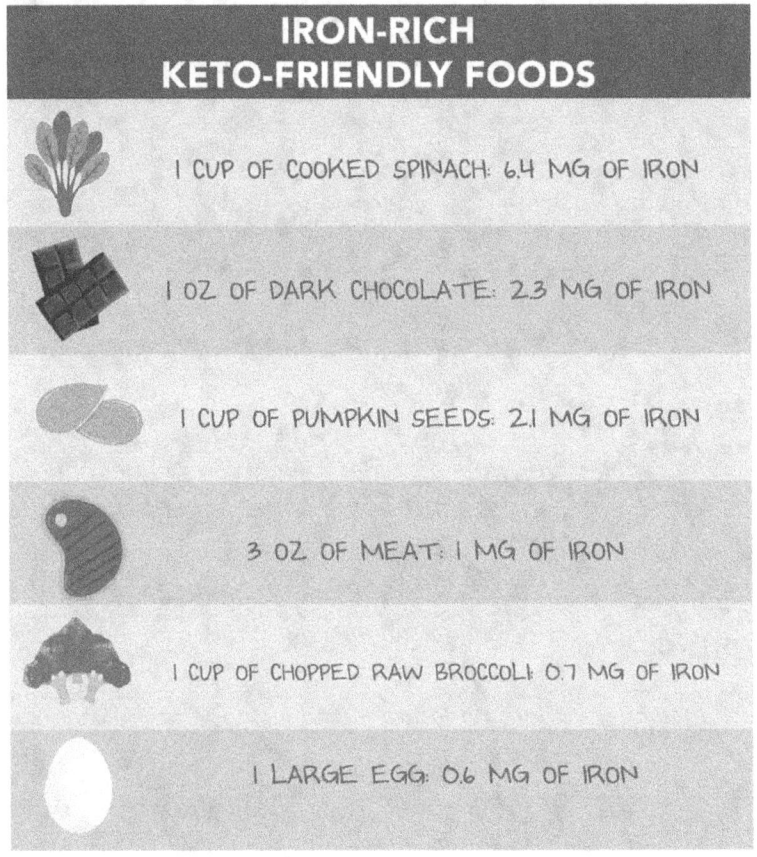

Phosphorous

Phosphorus helps to improve the cellular functions in your body by balancing your hormones, boosting your energy levels, improving your digestion, and helping to improve the efficiency of your body's utilization of nutrients.

When your body is experiencing a deficiency in phosphorus, you can begin to feel anxious, have trouble concentrating, experience tooth decay, and your bones can become weak.

In order to avoid this deterioration, you should try to have at least 700 milligrams of phosphorus every day. Fortunately, phosphorous deficiencies are very uncommon. You don't have to worry about tracking your intake of it as long as you eat a reasonable amount of broccoli, almonds, or eggs.

Vitamin A

Vitamin A is used for multiple bodily functions including vision, organ growth, and cellular reproduction. Like phosphorus, you don't have to worry too much about becoming deficient in Vitamin A.

It's commonly found in the ketogenic diet in the form of kale, spinach, fish, eggs, dairy, and broccoli.

Vitamin C

Vitamin C is an antioxidant that can prevent cholesterol from damaging your body tissue. It's also used to create collagen to strengthen muscles and blood vessels. Vitamin C deficiencies can cause scurvy—think sailors and pirates. Thankfully, we only need 10mg of vitamin C to keep scurvy at bay; this can easily be done without consuming any citrus fruit whatsoever.

Citrus fruits are notoriously high in carbohydrates. Fortunately, there are plenty of other foods that contain vitamin C that are keto-friendly. Consider getting your vitamin C from foods like broccoli, spinach, cauliflower, Brussels sprouts, and kale.

Vitamin K

Vitamin K is one of the lesser-known vitamins, but it plays an essential function. It's used to transport the calcium from your blood into your bones.

It's also used to assist in blood coagulation when you get a wound. If you are eating a lot of leafy greens on the keto diet, then you don't need to worry about your vitamin K consumption at all.

If you choose instead to fill up on bacon and eggs, then you're still fine—they contain vitamin K too.

Zinc

The enzymes found in zinc are used for healing wounds, cellular reproduction, and protein synthesis. With low levels of zinc in your body, you could have a harder time recovering from an injury or a workout.

Fortunately, zinc is easy to consume on the keto diet. It's found in everything from vegetables and mushrooms to less vegan-friendly products like poultry, meat, fish, and dairy.

Trying to Find Foods with Micronutrients vs. Supplements

For most people, it's always better to consume micronutrients through a food source. When they're naturally occurring, they tend to be more potent.

In addition, natural foods also tend to contain other accompanying substances like flavonoids, carotenoids, and antioxidants that assist the micronutrients in their processes and can't be found in supplements. Supplements were not designed as a substitute for food.

When you eat whole foods, you consume a much larger variety of nutrients, as well as fiber and antioxidants. Since your body has to take more time and energy to digest these substances, it tends to excrete them more slowly than supplements that have a tendency to show up in large levels in urine.

The quality of the food you eat plays a large role in its effectiveness as well. The more healthy and organic the food is, the more it tends to be dense with micronutrients.

This concentration is possibly due to the healthier growing conditions for organic foods. They are typically grown with the use of few pesticides and no hormones. Plus, they go through a rigorous process where they are graded for quality.

One great example of high-quality food making a difference is in the case of grass-fed beef. A single serving of grass-fed beef can contain more than six times the level of Omega-3 fatty acids than a serving of grain-fed beef.[13] Similar studies have also shown that fruits and vegetables raised naturally (like apples, broccoli, and carrots) have higher levels of antioxidants found in them.

When to Start Taking Supplements

While it's best to eat whole plants for nutrition, there are also times when it may be necessary for you to take a supplement to ensure your needs are being met.

Consider using a supplement if you:
- Are pregnant and having difficulty sustaining a complete diet
- You are above the age of fifty
- You don't get a lot of sun
- You are significantly reducing your calories
- You don't plan to eat a diverse diet of vegetables, meats, and fish
- You are vegetarian
- You have a medical condition that prevents your body from proper nutrient absorption

How Micronutrients Will Be Key to Your Keto Journey Success

The more balanced your diet is, the less susceptible you are to conditions like the keto flu.
As a way to avoid symptoms altogether, you may want to consider taking supplements at the beginning of your diet.

Try to buy supplements that are sourced from whole foods, and in an organic way, for the best results. Also, avoid eating foods that have little to no micronutrient value and a high-calorie content.

Foods like butter and vegetable oil may leave you feeling full, but they do little to support your body's health.

---

[13] Daley, Cynthia A et al. "A review of fatty acid profiles and antioxidant content in grass-fed and grain-fed beef." *Nutrition journal* vol. 9 10. 10 Mar. 2010, doi:10.1186/1475-2891-9-10

Before you start your keto journey, you may want to visit your doctor for an initial nutritional evaluation. They will be able to tell you where your existing vitamin levels stand so that you can make the right choices for yourself as you start to treat your body better.

Chapter Nine: Calculating Your Macros for the First Time

There are three macronutrients that the keto diet revolves around managing - fats, proteins, and carbohydrates.

To begin to understand how much of each of these nutrients your body needs, you have to start with the amount of calories you want to consume in a day.

Calories are a measure of energy. Every day you go to food as a figurative bank to get your energy currency. Then, you spend the entire day engaging in tasks that will make you spend that energy currency. If at the end of the day you have some spare energy change, it will get pocketed in your fat cells for a later time when you are short on energy currency.

If you are looking to lose weight, you will need to dip into those energy stores and use that as your currency for your daily tasks. This is where the keto diet comes in.

The keto diet is very good at making you feel full on fewer calories. This makes it easier for your body to dip into your fat cells and use them for energy. This is how you lose weight.

When you start the keto diet, it is important that you give your body all of the energy that it needs to adapt to this new fat-based metabolism. Once it is adapted, you can then ease into a lower-calorie diet for extra weight loss. It is, however, important to know that if you eat too little protein on the keto diet, you will end up losing bone mass along with the pounds. Protein always stays at the same amount, while you reduce calories from fat and carbohydrates.[14]

---

[14] Soleimani, Manoocher Insulin resistance and hypertension: new insights
Kidney International, Volume 87, Issue 3, 497 - 499

Calculate Your Basal Metabolic Rate

Since calculating your macros starts with the amount of calories you need to consume in a day, it's important that you calculate your basal metabolic rate first (BMR).

Go online and you will find automatic BMR calculators. Your BMR is a measure of the amount of calories it takes for your body to perform its natural activities like breathing and temperature regulation without any exercise or additional activity.

The higher your BMR, the more likely you are to need additional calories to support your body's basic functioning. It's nearly impossible to get an exact calculation for your BMR without visiting a dietary professional.

But, you can get close by using the Harris-Benedict equation.

For Men: BMR = 66 + (6.2 x Your weight in pounds) + (12.7 x Your height in inches) - (4.7 x Your age)

For Women: BMR = 655.1 + (4.35 x Your weight in pounds) + (4.7 x Your height in inches) - (4.7 x Your age)

Once you know your basal metabolic rate, you will have accounted for all of the calories you need to support your body's basic processes during the day. But, you still need to factor in the amount of energy you use in a day.

Calculate Your Total Daily Energy Expenditure

Your total daily energy expenditure (TDEE) is a measure of all of the activity you perform in one day. By multiplying your TDEE by your BMR, you can figure out a reasonable estimate of the amount of calories you need to consume in a given day.[15]

If you get little to no exercise, you should multiply your BMR by **1.2**.

If you perform light exercise, one to three days a week, you should multiply your BMR by **1.375**.

---

[15] Lam, Yan Y, and Eric Ravussin. "Analysis of energy metabolism in humans: A review of methodologies." *Molecular metabolism* vol. 5,11 1057-1071. 20 Sep. 2016, doi:10.1016/j.molmet.2016.09.005

If you perform moderate exercise three to five days a week, you should multiply your BMR by **1.55**.

For athletes who exercise six to seven days a week, the BMR should be multiplied by **1.725**.
For athletes who exercise multiple times a day, the BMR should be multiplied by **1.9**.

For example, if your BMR is 2,000 calories a day and your activity level is mild, you should multiply 2,000 x 1.375. Your answer is 2,750 calories a day.

Now that you have selected a number that corresponds to your energy level and multiplied it by your BMR, you know exactly how many calories per day your body needs to run at optimal levels.

Familiarize Yourself with Your Body Type

Knowing your body fat percentage can help you figure out how much protein you will need in order to support your musculoskeletal system. If your body is highly muscular, you will want to add more protein into your diet. If your body is higher in fat, you can keep a regular protein intake.

Calculating Your Carbohydrate Intake

When you are on a keto diet, you will take in a lot less carbohydrates than the average person. In fact, carbs will account for only about 5-10 percent of the total amount of calories you consume each day.

Note: Each gram of carb you count must be a net carb. This means that you subtract the amount of fiber listed on the label from the amount of carbohydrates before adding them into your daily calculation.

To figure out exactly how many carbohydrates you want to eat in one day, you should take the number you calculated (BMI x your TDEE) and multiply it by 0.05 (5 percent). Then, multiply your starting number by 0.10 (10 percent) to create a range for your daily carbohydrate consumption.

For example, based on this equation, if you are attempting to eat 2,000 calories a day, you will need 100 to 200 of those calories to come from carbs. You can then take that number and divide it by 4 (the amount of calories in a gram of carbs) to figure out that you should be eating between 25 to 50g of carbs each day.

Calculating Your Protein Intake

Consuming protein is the only way your body can create muscle mass. Eating too little protein can result in loss of muscle mass and bone density if you're not careful.[16]

Most people on the keto diet consume about 20 to 30 percent of their calories from protein. This will vary based on your body type, activity level, and weight loss objectives. The more active you are and the more muscle you want to gain, the more protein you should be eating.

Since you already calculated your body mass earlier, you can use that figure to calculate your optimal protein intake. You will need to figure out what percentage of your body is lean muscle mass. If you estimate that your body fat percentage is 25 percent, then you will want to account for 75 percent of your body weight when you make your protein calculation.

For example, a 175-lb person with 25 percent body fat would have about 130 pounds of lean body mass.

If you live a fairly sedentary lifestyle, you should try to have at least 0.6 grams of protein for every pound of lean body mass you have.[17]

That means our 175-lb person would consume around 80g of protein a day if they were sedentary. If they were active, this number could rise to more than 1g per pound. At that rate, they would need to consume 130g of protein in order to maintain their muscle mass.

Calculating Your Fat Intake

Now that you know how much protein and carbohydrates to eat, the only number left in your equation is your fat intake.

On the keto diet, fat will account for about 70 percent of the calories that you eat. Once you have subtracted your protein and carbohydrate needs from your total calorie needs for the day, all that's left is the amount of fat you need to consume.

---

[16] Lam, Yan Y, and Eric Ravussin. "Analysis of energy metabolism in humans: A review of methodologies." *Molecular metabolism* vol. 5,11 1057-1071. 20 Sep. 2016, doi:10.1016/j.molmet.2016.09.005
[17] Wu G. Dietary protein intake and human health. Food & function. 2016; 7(3):1251-65.

This 70 percent value is really more of a common value. For those who are adapted to the keto diet and are eating at a calorie deficit, this 70 percent value may drop while their protein percentage goes up.

In order to meet this number, you will need to include food with naturally occurring fats like avocados, salmon, and steak, etc.

Chapter Ten: Keto and Its Influence on Your Overall Health

For every article you read on the keto diet, there are both critics and supporters. There are diabetes patients who have been able to completely discontinue their medication and epileptic patients who no longer have seizure symptoms.

There are people who have lost tons of weight on the diet and those who hardly see a difference in their waistline. There are some who see their energy levels rise to new heights and others who feel sluggish and tired relying on ketones when they eat at a calorie deficit for too long.

There are people who will tell you to start the keto diet as soon as possible no matter who you are, while there are others who claim it's only useful for a small subset of the population. And for each of these people with an opinion, there are thousands more out there who either agree or disagree with them.

The fact of the matter is, everyone's body is different, and you don't really know how you're going to feel on a keto diet until you try it.

What we do know is that keto diets are nutritionally sound, and they are a reasonably healthy way to attempt weight loss. We also know that they have been scientifically proven to have positive effects on a wide variety of health conditions.

Always consult your doctor first. That said, you should have very little fear in starting a keto diet—especially after reading this guide. Calculate your macros, purchase the right ingredients, and give it an honest try.

Chapter Eleven: The Keto Flu

Although the first couple of days on the keto diet will be very fun and exciting, there's one challenge that many people face and that is the "keto flu."

You might begin to feel tired, fatigued, have stomach pains, and become dizzy. These symptoms are common and harmless, so don't worry—you're just passing a checkpoint.

These symptoms come from the challenge of restricting carbohydrates because your body is used to relying on carbohydrates for quick pick-me-ups of energy. You might call it carb-withdrawals, so to speak.

After all, carbs are very comforting to eat; they're sweet, fluffy, and warm. But, those good feelings you experience in the moment of consumption are quickly replaced by inconsistent energy levels and increased weight gain.

There are plenty of keto-friendly food items that will give you the same consolatory feeling, so trust the process. Breaking up with carbs is a great idea for your body and your waistline.

Before you get overwhelmed and decide keto isn't for you, remember that in order to start processing ketones rather than carbohydrates, your body will need a period of time to adapt. It's going to be challenging at first.

You may have cravings and wonder how you will make it. But after a couple of days, your amazing body will have adjusted completely and you'll be feeling like your normal self—probably even better.

Common Symptoms of the Keto Flu

The symptoms can start as soon as the first day and can last anywhere from two days to more than a week.

Many people experience intense cravings, feelings of dizziness, fogginess of the mind, increased irritability, an inability to concentrate, stomach pains, nausea, insomnia, muscle soreness, and cramping.

Fortunately, most people don't develop all of these symptoms at the same time. How you experience the keto flu varies. This is because everyone's metabolic system is different. If your body generally has good metabolic flexibility, it can adapt to different fuel sources more quickly.

Imagine the keto flu as an honorific rite of passage; the harder the keto flu hits, the more you need the keto diet.

For those who are less metabolically flexible, it can take as long as a month to fully adjust to the keto diet. Your rate of metabolic flexibility generally comes down to genetics and lifestyle choices.

While there is little you can do about your genetics, there is a lot you can do to create a solid lifestyle for starting a keto diet. Before you adopt the diet completely, you can prime your body by reducing your intake of refined sugars and carbohydrates beforehand.

You can also defeat the keto flu by adding more exercise into your routine. Exercise forces your body to become more metabolically flexible sooner. By putting pressure on your body's energy extraction system, you can speed up the process and end your keto flu symptoms.

More Tips for the Keto Flu

Having a proper understanding of the keto flu can help you avoid some of its symptoms. Let's look at some tips for kicking the keto flu before it begins.

1.   Hydrate and Get Enough Electrolytes

Make sure you drink plenty of water and supplement your diet with additional sodium and other electrolytes when you first begin the keto diet.

When you begin to restrict your carbohydrate consumption, you remove one of the major triggers for insulin release in your body. Insulin is used to help your body shuttle glucose into your bloodstream. But, it also sends a signal to your kidneys, letting them know to hold on to sodium and water.

If your insulin levels are too low, sodium will be released from your body and will take a lot of water with it. This is why many people lose a lot of weight during the first few days of the keto diet. Low insulin and glycogen levels can lead to common keto flu symptoms like dizziness and nausea, as well as cramping and headaches.

2. **Eat More Fat**

To help your body adapt to the keto diet quickly, you have to help it along by giving it enough fat.

Make sure you calculate your macros accurately and fulfill your body's daily caloric needs. If you don't get enough calories, you'll be destined to feel shaky and tired. Eat up now.

3. **Consider Low-Intensity Exercises in the Morning**

Start your first day on the keto diet by grabbing a bottle of water and putting a pinch of sodium-rich salt into it. Then, take a long walk to get your metabolism going.

Walk at a quick pace that gets your heart rate going but that doesn't make you out of breath. Try to continue that rate for about an hour. The longer you walk, the better you should feel.

You will also begin to feel more energized and awake. Although you're only engaging in low-impact exercise, it can have a profound effect on your body's ability to burn fat and switch over to a ketogenic state.

This simple step alone can prevent you from experiencing many of the common symptoms of the keto flu. If you find that the exercise is taxing, you may just be dehydrated or not eating enough. Run through your calculations again while you chug a glass of water.

4. **Meditate and Maintain a Positive Outlook**

The changes in your body can make you feel more stressed and irritated than normal. To help slow down your body's shock, it can be helpful to start meditating.

Consider sitting in silence for fifteen minutes every day. Use this time to take deep breaths and focus your mind on relaxation. Meditation can help increase your positive outlook on the keto diet. This is not something you are doing to yourself as punishment. It's something you're doing for yourself and your future.

5. Prioritize Your Sleep

Make sure you are getting a full seven to nine hours of sleep each night. If you add in a thirty minute nap or fifteen minute meditation session, it might also help you re-center throughout the day. Of course, these are known tips for well-being in general. Keep in mind you are changing your lifestyle.

Chapter Twelve: Keto and Fasting

Intermittent fasting is a huge trend in the weight-loss and nutrition world and it's been around since the beginning of mankind.

Intermittent fasting can be a great way to supplement your keto diet. This practice involves scheduling your food intake for optimal times of day. Eating a healthy diet isn't just about what you consume; when you eat and how often are also important factors to consider.

There are three common ways to go about intermittent fasting. Some people choose to skip meals to introduce their bodies to a fasting state. Many people skip breakfast, while others choose to forfeit dinner.

Other people try to create eating windows for themselves. With this style of diet, you will eat within a four- to eight-hour window every day. During this time, you will need to take in all of the macronutrients you will need for the day.

The third common kind of fast is a twenty-four to forty-eight-hour cleanse. This is similar to a religious fast where you do not eat anything for one to two days. Intermittent fasting is popular for keto dieters because their bodies are already less dependent on constant caloric intakes for energy.

Your system is already burning its existing stores. For most people, a one- to two-day fast is not necessary, but can be explored after a few months on the keto diet. If you do choose to try an extended fast, it is very important that you do your grocery shopping beforehand. This way, when you choose to break it, you will not be tempted by processed foods, and you will already have your meal planned.

After all, when our hunter-gatherer ancestors would break their fast, it would be with whatever they'd hunted or gathered.

Intermittent Fasting and Overeaters

Intermittent fasting can be great for people who tend to overeat. If you can increase the amount of food you eat at one time of day, it's easier to keep track of. And, our bodies can only accommodate so much food at one time.

If you can decrease your eating window, and you usually snack throughout the day, you're destined to lose weight. You will no longer have to worry about counting and monitoring your snacks. You just eat inside your window.

While intermittent fasting may be difficult at first, you will be able to record and maintain your nutritional values more easily. Over time, your body will begin to adjust to your fasts and you will no longer feel hungry, tired, or irritable.

Fasting and Willpower

When choosing any form of diet, educate yourself first on the kind of people who are successful on that diet. Talk to your doctor about how your body is set up similarly or differently from others to make sure a diet trend is right for you. Then, give it a try and stick with it—or, at least try to.

Let's say you're used to eating breakfast first thing in the morning. Why not try to extend that time by one hour over the course of three days?

It may take trying several variations of the keto diet to be able to find the one that works for your body. Don't be afraid to make changes and learn more about why you're having difficulty with your weight loss. There may be barriers to overcome, but if you persevere, the results you desire will come to you.

Chapter Thirteen: Keto in the Grocery Store and in the Kitchen

Shopping trips will no longer be about wandering the aisles and filling your basket with junk. Say hello to the most glorious beef brisket you've ever made, the cheesiest western you've ever had, and to precious avocados, wondrous salmon, and some good old crispy chicken.

Entering the grocery store will be delightful because you will no longer be wasting your time and money on regretful purchases. Now you will have a purpose.

Let's take a look at some of the biggest adjustments you'll make in the way you approach your local market, as well as food prep in the kitchen.

Keto in the Grocery Store

Your primary stops will be the deli, seafood counter, meat counter, dairy case, frozen aisle, and produce section. Here are some more tips for shopping at the grocery store.

1. Banish "Light" or "Lite" Variations from Your Shopping List

While you may have been raised to opt for the reduced-fat or low-fat version of things like sour cream, butter, and milk, you are now going to need to reach for the full-fat version. Yummy.

In fact, go ahead and banish all of the items on your grocery list that are described as "light." From now on, you're all about full-fat flavor.

And, if you can't find a full-fat yogurt, then purchase the low-fat version; later, you'll add in heavy cream or creme fraiche. Some keto dieters choose to avoid yogurts altogether though because of their high sugar content.

But, the thicker the yogurt that you choose, the less carbohydrates it will contain. Try to opt for options like Greek yogurt that also contain good amounts of protein.

2. Consider Online Ordering

When you visit a grocery store in person, it may be difficult to walk past the chip aisle and away from the bakery. That bag of chips that you buy for your kid's lunches could end up becoming your midnight snack if you're not careful.

But, with online shopping, you can remove a lot of the temptation that lies in wait at the grocery store. Instead of being seduced by the cookies and breads in the bakery, you can just enter the items you need into your search bar.

Consider ordering keto-friendly items online and having them delivered right to your doorstep. You may be concerned about not being able to pick out the produce and meat yourself, but you will find that many people who shop with delivery services frequently receive high-quality items.

Companies know that you have a lot of options when you shop, and they are familiar with the complaint of bruised or overly ripe produce. They will do everything they can to ensure the freshest ingredients possible end up at your doorstep. If you notice an issue with items coming from one company, simply try another service.

3. Choose Fattier Cuts of Meat

Getting enough fat naturally in the meat that you eat is a great way to maintain your diet and to stay feeling full throughout the day. The fattier it is, the less you will feel hungry later.

To ensure you consume all of the fat within your meat, try to choose cuts that are marbled, with the fat evenly dispersed throughout. Don't just look for cuts of meat that have large chunks of fat hanging off of them.

4. Select Fatty Pieces of Fish and Seafood

The same rules that apply to meat also apply to fish. Try to opt for fattier cuts of fish like salmon, rather than leaner options like tilapia. You'll notice that the filet will be more filling and tastier. You'll also remain full and satisfied longer.

5. Look Up Low-Carb Recipes in Advance

Some stores are nice and have an easy-to-spot section for low-carb items. But, many grocery stores haven't adjusted to the trend yet, and it will take a little bit more guidance for you to make the right selections.

For that reason, it's important that you create a grocery list based on low-carb recipes before you go to the grocery store. It's much less stressful to sit down at home and plan out your meals than to rack your brain in the middle of an aisle.

6. Stock Your Refrigerator with Real, Whole Foods

One of your favorite places to shop when you're on the keto diet will be the produce aisle. Many keto dieters place no limit on the amount of non-starchy vegetables that they can eat in a day.

So, feel free to load up your cart with these vegetables:
- Arugula
- Artichokes

- Asparagus
- Broccoli
- Bok choy
- Brussel sprouts
- Cabbage
- Cauliflower
- Eggplant
- Green beans
- Garlic
- Kale
- Lettuce
- Leeks
- Mushrooms
- Mustard greens
- Onions
- Peppers
- Shallots
- Summer squash
- Swiss chard
- Spinach
- Tomatoes
- Zucchini

While you're still in the produce section, you may also want to stock up on fresh herbs like basil, mint, oregano, cilantro, and parsley.

These items can offer a lot of additional flavor to the foods you cook and can also be added to your water to make hydration more exciting.

We all know that fruits are considered to be healthy. However, they aren't part of the keto diet; they can completely ruin ketosis. Be restrictive with fruit—you don't want to go overboard with the amount of fructose you consume. If you do choose to eat fruit, make it no more than once a week. Try to reach for fruits that have the lowest amount of sugar possible, like berries and some melons.

Keto in the Kitchen

Let's start with some simple rules to follow to help you get started.

1. Always Include a Solid Protein Source
In order to feel full and have your body functioning at its best, eating protein with every meal is super important. To start your day with a low-carb breakfast, consider choosing eggs for an inexpensive and quick option. Don't forget, there's also bacon, steak, sausage, ham, and turkey as well.

At lunch and dinner time, you should choose high-quality cuts of fatty meat that were raised on grass in a pasture. They will contain more omega-3 fatty acids than other pieces of meat. If you don't have time for a complete meal at lunch or dinner, you can opt for something like sliced turkey or canned tuna for a quick pick-me-up. You may also want to purchase snack meats like beef jerky. Just make sure you choose a natural brand that is low in sodium and sugar.

2. Cook with Fats like Butter and Oil
If you want your food to have good flavor and to keep you full for a long time, it's key that it's cooked in a lot of butter and oil. Avoid seed oils because they are inflammatory and cause metabolic dysfunction.

3. Switch Up Your Fat Source for Flavor Enhancement
If you find yourself getting bored of the basics, like olive oil and butter, you may want to opt for some new oil sources in your life. Consider trying other healthy oils like avocado and coconut oil.

4. Don't Forget the Spices
Changing the oils you use to cook your food can alter the flavor a lot. Without spices, howver, your food will be bland. So, let's season it up, shall we?

I've already recommended that you fill your grocery cart with lots of fresh herbs to enhance your cooking. Don't let them go bad in your refrigerator—use them.

You can also create pockets of herbs and store them in tinfoil in your freezer. Before you start prepping for any meal, consider what herbs you might be able to use in the dish and cut them up in advance. Or, grab them from your freezer pockets. Not only will they add flavor to your dish, but they are also packed with essential nutrients.

5. Top Your Dishes with Olive Oil

Another great way to make the transition from weight loss to stabilized weight is to add olive oil as a topping to pretty much all of your dishes. This is a common practice in Mediterranean cooking. Just make sure you measure the amount of oil you are adding so that you don't go overboard on your drizzle.

6. Add a Fat Source to Your Coffee

This tip also applies to when you have reached your target weight on the keto diet and are looking to reintroduce some calories. Adding a fat source to your coffee (like butter or almond milk) can help give you a jump-start on your calories for the day.

Starting your day with a cup of coffee like this can make you feel full and focused for several hours. If you have trouble losing weight though, do not do this.

7. Throw in a Cheese Course

While dairy and dairy products are technically permitted on the keto diet, they always come with an asterisk next to them. Some options are healthier for your diet than others. Try to avoid flavored milks that are high in sugar.

Instead, opt for full-fat cream options. You can also fill your cart with cottage cheese, sour cream, and butter.

Cheese courses can also provide a good source of dairy and nutrients on the keto diet while adding a bit of flavor to your meal. Try to opt for harder cheeses that are low in sugar.

Chapter Fourteen: What is Diabetes and How Can Keto Help?

Type 2 diabetes is a chronic disease that prevents your body from using insulin properly. The proper term for the disease is "insulin resistant."

People who are around middle age tend to start seeing higher rates of insulin diabetes, leading to its nickname, "adult-onset diabetes." But, this name is a misnomer. Type 2 diabetes can affect children and teens who struggle with their weight and obesity.

Type 2 diabetes is the most common form, and there are around twenty-nine million people in the United States struggling to manage their insulin resistance. There are also another eighty-four million people who are pre-diabetic, which means that they are on their way to developing the disease. Most people don't even know they're pre-diabetic because their blood sugar levels aren't yet high enough to be considered diabetes.[18]

How You Can Tell You Have Type 2 Diabetes

Type 2 diabetes symptoms can often be very mild. In fact, there are most likely millions of people living with the disease who don't even know that they have it.

Some of the major symptoms include:
- Feeling tired and fatigued
- Peeing frequently
- Excessive thirst
- Blurry vision
- Crankiness
- Tingling and numbness in your hands and feet
- Wounds that have trouble healing

---

[18] Rebolledo, Julio A, and Regina Arellano. "Cultural Differences and Considerations When Initiating Insulin." *Diabetes spectrum : a publication of the American Diabetes Association* vol. 29,3 (2016): 185-90. doi:10.2337/diaspect.29.3.185

- Recurring yeast infections
- Excessive hunger
- Weight loss without effort
- Increase in proneness to infection
- Dark rashes in the neck and armpit area

Causes of Type 2 Diabetes

Insulin, made in the pancreas, is the carrier that lets sugar into our cells via the bloodstream. This is how your cells get energy.

You get glucose from food that has been metabolized, and that metabolized glucose floats around in your gut, and then gets transported into the bloodstream through the intestinal cells.

Once the glucose is in the bloodstream, insulin comes in to pull that glucose into the cells of the body to feed those cells.

Type 2 diabetes, or insulin resistant diabetes, is when the cells of the body are not receptive to the insulin that is trying to push the glucose in. So, that glucose is stuck in the bloodstream and causes the physiological response of type 2 diabetes. When insulin cannot properly allow the blood glucose from the bloodstream into the cell, the glucose stays in the bloodstream, meaning that there is a high blood sugar level.

Genes

Type 2 diabetes can be caused by a variety of circumstances. Some scientists believe that it is linked to your genes. There are several parts of our DNA that give instructions for the way our bodies make insulin.

If your DNA instructions aren't optimal, you could develop the condition over time. But, don't let your family history of type 2 diabetes get you down. It's a very manageable condition, and it's preventable with a healthy diet and exercise routine.

Extra Weight

Another risk factor for type 2 diabetes is extra weight. The more overweight you are, the more resistant to insulin your body can become. This is particularly true for overweight people who have a lot of body fat on their torso.

Metabolic Syndrome

Metabolic syndrome is a term for the grouping of conditions associated with people suffering from insulin resistance. It includes high blood pressure, high blood sugar, additional fat at the waist, high cholesterol, type 2 diabetes, and triglycerides.

Too Much Liver Glucose

Type 2 diabetes can also develop when too much glucose is made and sent out by the liver. When you eat, your blood sugar levels typically rise. At that time, your liver will choose to slow down its release of glucose and reserve it for later.

But, when you have type 2 diabetes, your liver keeps putting out sugar, causing it to rise in your blood levels and make you ill.

Bad Cell Signals

Poor intercellular communication can affect the amount of insulin or glucose in your body. If your body sends the wrong signals, it can end in a chain reaction that causes diabetes.

Broken Beta Cells

Beta cells are the cells that make insulin. When they send out an incorrect amount of insulin at a time that isn't optimal, it can throw off your blood sugar levels. This problem is a feedback loop because, in turn, the high levels of blood sugar will damage the beta cells further.

Risk Factors for Type 2 Diabetes

There are several factors that can make you more prone to developing type 2 diabetes. The more factors that apply to you, the more likely you are to get the disease.

People over the age of forty-five are at a higher risk than the general population of developing type 2 diabetes. Another major risk factor is genetics. If you have a parent, brother, or sister that has diabetes, then you are more likely to get it.

There are also certain ethnicities in the general population that seem to be more prone to developing type 2 diabetes including:

- African Americans
- Native Alaskans
- Native Americans
- Asian Americans
- Hispanics and Latinos
- Pacific Islanders

Other risk factors for type 2 diabetes are those that relate to your medical history and general health.

You're at a heightened risk for developing type 2 diabetes if you:
- Have been diagnosed with prediabetes
- Have had cardiovascular disease
- Have had high blood pressure, even if it's currently controlled
- Have had low levels of good (HDL) cholesterol
- Have had high triglyceride levels
- Are overweight
- Have given birth to a baby over nine pounds
- Have developed gestational diabetes during pregnancy
- Have polycystic ovarian syndrome
- Have been depressed

The following risk factors for developing type 2 diabetes concern the way you live your daily life. This is the section of risk factors where you have the most control.

If you eat too many carbs, don't get enough exercise, smoke, have a lot of stress, or sleep too little, then you just may develop type 2 diabetes.

Ways to Manage Type 2 Diabetes

Once it develops, there are several different ways to manage your type 2 diabetes. The first is by making lifestyle changes, like losing weight. If you can lose just 7 percent of your body weight and keep it off, you will have healthier blood sugar levels.[19]

Weight loss may seem like an overwhelming plan, but with proper portion control and the right foods, you will be well on your way to defeating type 2 diabetes. Another great way to attack the problem is with exercise.

The United States Department of Health and Human Services recommends that Americans get at least one hundred fifty minutes of moderate intensity physical activity at least two days per week. They also recommend that youth get at least sixty minutes of physical activity every day.[20]

Another way people manage their type 2 diabetes is with medication. This is because moderate lifestyle changes alone are rarely enough to achieve target blood sugar levels. But, adding a ten-minute walk after a meal to your daily routine can be enough of a change for many people to manage their blood sugar levels. It may even work better than a prescription for Metformin, a well-known diabetes drug.

How the Keto Diet Can Help

The keto diet has historically been used to manage insulin levels in the body. It can help you manage both your insulin resistance and any excess weight issues you may be dealing with.[21]

Frequently Asked Questions

What should I tell people about my keto diet?

---

[19] Khatri, M. (2019, November 6). Type 2 Diabetes: Symptoms, Causes, Diagnosis, and Treatment. Retrieved from https://www.webmd.com/diabetes/type-2-diabetes#1

[20] Adapted from U.S. Department of Health and Human Services. 2008 Physical Activity Guidelines for Americans. Washington (DC): U.S. Department of Health and Human Services; 2008. Available at: http://www.health.gov/paguidelines. Accessed August 6, 2015.

[21] Yancy, W.S., Foy, M., Chalecki, A.M. et al. A low-carbohydrate, ketogenic diet to treat type 2 diabetes. Nutr Metab (Lond) 2, 34 (2005). https://doi.org/10.1186/1743-7075-2-34

In a social context, many people are embarrassed to admit they are on a diet or are trying to lose weight and change their appearance. Don't force the topic of your diet. But, if it does come up, there are a few things you can be prepared with. For starters, most people are usually quite accepting of personal experiments. All you would have to say is that you're trying out this new way of eating by cutting out processed sugars and that you're trying to eat more whole foods that come from meats and vegetables. If whoever you're with expresses skepticism, just let them know that you'll try something different if this doesn't work for you. But, you want to give this way of eating a good effort for at least two to three months.

You may even be pleasantly surprised and find that the keto movement is quite popular. Even if your entourage isn't eating exactly like you are, it might surprise you to find that you're probably not the only one trying to cut back on carbs. Keep an eye out for other low-carb eaters.

If people are asking about what you're eating, it might be because they're interested in the keto diet as well. Be a voice of reason and share your experiences.

Who does best on the keto diet?

The keto diet is for everyone! Those who see the best results are those who are looking to lose weight. But, the keto diet can help anyone take control of their eating habits. Most often, the keto diet is recommended by healthcare workers who are familiar with its weight loss benefits. The diet is particularly good for overweight individuals who are struggling with metabolic syndrome, insulin resistance, and type 2 diabetes.

People suffering from these kinds of conditions often see improvement in the clinical markers for their diseases when they engage in a low-carb diet.[22]

Does the keto diet help you lose weight?

Many people see successful weight loss on the keto diet during their first three to six months. These changes stem from the fact that it takes more calories of energy to turn fat into ready fuel for your body than it does to use carbohydrates for the same purpose.

---

[22] Feinman, R. D. (2015, January). Dietary carbohydrate restriction: Compelling theory for further research. https://www.sciencedirect.com/science/article/abs/pii/S089990071500115X

Another aspect of the keto diet that makes it helpful for weight loss is that many people find the diet to be satiating. When you eat a lot of fat and protein, you can eat less while still feeling full.

The keto diet has also been proven to help you improve your blood sugar levels throughout the day. You will no longer suffer with the energy level ups and downs that come with eating carbs.
Without these energy crashes, you will no longer feel the immense hunger that comes from an empty stomach that is craving more carbohydrates.

Instead, you will have more consistent blood sugar levels regardless of what keto food you eat. Because of this feeling of fullness, you may choose to start keto fasting cycles. You'll simply find it easier to jump into since your body won't feel as shocked from food withdrawl.

Can the keto diet help protect your body from cancer?

There are some articles in circulation that claim a keto diet can help keep your body cancer-free. While there may be some truth to these claims, little of it can be proven at this time.

The working theory is that since your body burns through so little sugar when you're on a keto diet, your body doesn't have to make as much insulin to store that sugar as fuel. Therefore, your body would need, and make, less insulin. The lower levels of insulin are theorized to convert to lower levels of cancer and slower growth rates of cancerous cells.

As the idea is explored more by scientists, more results will emerge either verifying or disproving this claim. Another effect the keto diet can have on cancer is giving the cancer cells less to feed on. Cancer cells like to feed on glucose to survive. The lower your glucose levels are, the more cancer treatment may be effective.[23] Fasting can also make cancer cells more vulnerable to treatment.[24]

What should you do if you are considering starting a keto diet for weight loss?

The best thing you can do if you are considering a keto diet for weight loss is to consult your doctor to ensure it's safe for you. While many people have successfully started and completed keto diets

---

[23] Weber DD, Aminazdeh-gohari S, Kofler B. Ketogenic diet in cancer therapy. Aging (Albany NY). 2018;10(2):164-165.
[24] De groot S, Pijl H, Van der hoeven JJM, Kroep JR. Effects of short-term fasting on cancer treatment. J Exp Clin Cancer Res. 2019;38(1):209.

without any problems, everyone's body is different. Your doctor will be able to evaluate your current metabolic state and give you a good idea of what to expect while on your diet.

Most people's doctors will immediately approve them for the keto diet. Even pregnant women can experience the benefits of going low-carb. But, if you are pregnant and on blood sugar medicine for diabetes, you may need to take particular care to visit your doctor.

If you choose to go keto, you may see major improvements in your blood sugar levels and there will be less of a fluctuation for your medication to manage. Because of this effect, your doctor may recommend that you cut back on your medication, or stop taking it altogether.

You should also reach out to friends and family members who have tried the keto diet. Many people have done a lot of research into this form of dieting and can talk through your expectations with you to make sure you're prepared for the transition. Just make sure that you talk to people who have tried the keto diet and stayed on it successfully.

Listening to too much naysaying from people who aren't qualified to talk about what really happens to your body on a keto diet can derail your progress. Finally, you will need to write a new master grocery list for what you will keep in your house at all times. While making fancy keto recipes online is great at mealtime, it won't do much for those times when you need a quick snack to help you get out the door on time to your evening classes or extracurricular practice.

Fortunately, keto diets are great because they keep you full in between meals, meaning you're less likely to have the urge to snack. Since you avoid the blood sugar crashes between meals, you may even feel less hungry.

How can you increase your odds of success on the keto diet?

In order to be successful on the keto diet, you need to be prepared both mentally and physically. Expectations are everything.

Many people believe starting a keto diet will be a relatively straightforward process. But you will need to place close attention to the way you are eating, when you are eating, and what you are eating if you want to maximize your weight loss.

1. Keep a Written Log

One of the best ways to manage your diet is by keeping a written chart where you log all of the carbs and calories that you eat. Although this isn't strictly necessary for losing weight on keto, it is definitely a method you can consider to ensure you are being consistent so that you will see results.

Many people find keeping a log to be too time-consuming. But, when you're first beginning the diet, it's a great way to stay organized. If you find yourself having a hard time keeping up with your log, you should focus your effort and attention on eating the right portions of fat and protein without overindulging in carbohydrates.

2. Be on the Lookout for Sneaky Carbs

When you're on the keto diet, it's okay to drink milk and consume dairy products in moderation. But, if you're not careful, consuming dairy can lead to too much carbohydrate consumption without you realizing it.

This is because many companies who produce these products choose to label them as 0 carbohydrates, even if they have 0.6g or less. This kind of deception is allowed on many different food labels in the United States. Be sure that you are doing your research to find out how many carbohydrates are truly in the products you are consuming.

3. Be Cautious of Dairy Products

Just because it's okay to drink some milk, does not mean that you should have much. One of the major energy sources in milk is lactose, which is a sugar. If you are going to consume dairy products, it's best to have hard cheeses that add a lot of flavor (but not a lot of lactose) to your diet.

4. Recalculate Your Macros as You Lose Weight

When you first start the keto diet, you will calculate the amount of each macronutrient that you should be eating based on your lifestyle habits and physical measurements. This amount is tailored to what you weigh and how your body is at the beginning of the process.

But, as you lose weight over time, your body's nutritional needs will begin to change. As that happens, you need to recalculate the amount of macronutrients you should be eating each day to account for your weight loss.

It's a good rule of thumb to readjust your macros every time you lose ten pounds. This way, you can continue to see the kind of progress on the scale that you have gotten used to.

If you find yourself struggling to count and track your macros regularly, you're not alone. Often times this responsibility is left to dieticians and healthcare providers for bodybuilders and highly-trained athletes.

As a general rule, focus on eating the right amount of protein every day, then eat some vegetables without over-stressing their carb content, and get the right amount of fat in your diet.

If you find yourself no longer losing weight, it's time to reduce your fat intake. You may want to cut back on the amount of oil or butter that you're cooking with.

5. Be Cautious with Seeds and Nuts

A lot of people think nuts and seeds will be keto-friendly simply because they are known for containing large amounts of protein and fat. But, unfortunately, they also have a lot of carbohydrates.

When you're on the keto diet, you can't turn to snacking on nuts throughout the day as a harmless option. The carbohydrates can add up over time. While it's not bad to use nuts as a garnish or as part of a recipe you're cooking, it's important not to turn to them as a snack substitute the way they're often used in other diets.

6. Ease into the Process

When you first start this process, you're going to find that the food might taste a little funny to you. You may think that it tastes too rich or oily. But, the longer you are on the diet, the more your body and your taste buds will adjust to the food.

If you find your food is oily, then you're most likely trying too hard to pack fat into your diet. Remember that there are 9 calories in every gram of fat. You'll be able to hit your fat goal very easily on the keto diet.

Don't forget, there are naturally occurring fats in a lot of the foods that you eat. You shouldn't need to add too much oil or butter to your meals in order to meet the recommended daily intake. The key is to get enough fat into your diet early on so that you won't become hungry.

You don't have to force yourself to eat an uncomfortable amount of fat, but you do have to increase your consumption as you continue with the process if you want to be successful. Try to give yourself a month to ease into the keto diet by adopting ketogenic foods at certain meals. You will need to cut your carbohydrate intake significantly at the same time, but you don't yet have to lower it to the levels necessary to enter ketosis if you're not ready.

But, also remember that the less strict you are with your diet in the beginning, the slower your progress will be at first. Some people choose to take the plunge and adopt the entire diet immediately so that they don't risk losing their motivation when they don't see the changes they are looking for in the mirror right away.

7. Cut Back for Extra Weight Loss

If you are seeing your progress stall on the keto diet, then you may want to re-examine your macro count or adjust the amount of fat you are adding to your meals. Your goal is to eat just the right amount you need to have in order to avoid being hungry.

Anything extra is just displacing the calories you could have been burning from your body's fat stores. Try to find the perfect balance in between maximizing your weight loss and ensuring your body has the proper amount of fuel for the day to avoid hunger.

8. When You Reach Your Goal, Reintroduce Fat Sources

Eventually, if you continue observing a strict keto diet, you will lose the weight you are trying to get rid of. This isn't some magical miracle pill. If you create a calorie deficit, your body will burn its caloric stores of fat to compensate. If you stick to the plan, success is on the horizon.

Once you get there, you're going to need to make some adjustments. If you want to keep the weight off, it's a good idea to continue to stick to a low-carb diet even after you've reached your goal.

You will need to start reintroducing more fat sources until you find yourself at a weight that is consistent and easy to maintain. Then, you've done it! You can keep eating that measured amount and know your weight won't fluctuate much.

Hopefully, by the time you reach your target weight on the diet, you will have a better understanding of the way your body processes food. You should have enough experience at that point to troubleshoot any weight you might gain and stop the increase before it becomes a problem.

If you've done everything right, then you won't have much of a need for that kind of experimentation once you've reached your weight loss goal. You should already be eating the right amount of nutrients for the body that you have.

Your goal is not to leave your body in a permanent state of calorie deficit. But, rather, to help you live a clean and natural lifestyle that leaves you feeling healthy and energized.

9. Make Sure You Get Enough Protein

If you find yourself in the midst of a bout of intense hunger, you're going to want to reach for the snack closest to you that's easiest to make. But, giving into cravings and snacking is not a way to achieve your goals. You need to focus on the big picture and set yourself up for success.

Fortunately, if you eat reasonably-sized meals on the keto diet, you shouldn't find yourself getting too hungry in between meals. If you do, it can be a sign that you need to eat more at meal time.

One way to ensure you never become too hungry is to get the right amount of protein every day. The requirement for everyone's body is different. But, on average, most people will lose weight if they are consuming about 1.5 grams of protein for every kilogram of their body weight.

For people who are highly active, this amount could be much higher. Consider your activity levels when selecting the amount of protein you will eat that day and opt for extra if you find yourself hungry after consuming a meal high in fats.

Can I drink alcohol on the keto diet?

It can be difficult to feel like you have a full social life on the keto diet. After all, not only do you have to look out for carbs in the foods that you eat, but also in everything that you drink.

Fortunately, you don't have to cut alcohol out altogether to be on a keto diet. But it certainly would help. Consider starting by cutting out all beer and wine. Stick to hard liquor that has fewer calories, carbohydrates, and sugar.

Although hard liquors are made from natural sugars and potatoes, these substances are broken down into ethyl alcohol during fermentation. In fact, drinking liquor can actually encourage the production of ketones in your liver, thus deepening the level of ketosis you are in.

Just be aware that you may become drunk more easily than when you're eating carbs. This is because the body is readily able to digest the alcohol. Take things slow at first, particularly if you plan on driving.

What are the least harmful kinds of alcohol to drink on the keto diet?

If you're going to drink, you might as well have something low in carbs and calories.

If beer is your drink of choice, you could choose:
- Bud Select
- Miller 64
- Michelob Ultra
- Other light beers that are low in carbs

If you prefer to drink wine, you want to opt for something that is unsweetened or unflavored. You may also want to try dry white or red wines. Unfortunately, even the lowest-carb wines still come out to be about a gram of carbs per ounce. Be careful how much you choose to indulge in wine if you're on a keto diet.

Liquor is by far your best option. All liquor has 0g net carbs, but has 7 calories per milliliter of pure alcohol. If your drink is at 7 percent alcohol, then 7 percent of your drink is pure alcohol and that alcohol content can be very caloric. Plus, the alcohol will need to be detoxified by the liver, and those suffering from metabolic diseases should avoid alcohol in order for them to avoid fatty liver disease. Just make sure you avoid the liqueurs and mixers that typically go with them. If you must have a mixer, opt for a carb-free soda water option.

Is fasting a good idea on the keto diet?

Intermittent fasting is a very popular trend for people on a variety of different diets. While it may seem dangerous to skip a meal, in actuality it can be quite healthy.

Intermittent fasting is a particularly good idea if you've started to hit a weight loss plateau on your diet. It can help you shed the last couple of pounds before you hit your target weight.

Another benefit of intermittent fasting is the way your metabolic system begins to adapt. You can begin to see increased muscle growth and protein synthesis. You will be able to see your body respond to a meal after a workout.

Some people claim that intermittent fasting helps them increase their mental clarity as well. There is more on intermittent fasting in Chapter Twelve of the e-book.

How do I reach ketosis?

Achieving ketosis is the entire point of practicing a keto diet. It may seem complicated before you attempt it, but reaching a ketogenic state is actually very straightforward.

As a bottom line, you have to make sure that you're restricting your carbohydrates. If you want to see truly amazing results, don't just focus on limiting your net carbs (carbohydrates minus fiber)—factor in the entire amount. Just make sure that you stay between 20 and 30g of carbs per day if you're trying to lose weight.

You should also try to stop worrying about fat. It's going to be your primary source of energy on the keto diet and it's what will make you feel full in between meals. If you don't eat enough fat on the keto diet, you're destined to fail.

To reach ketosis, you will also need to drink a lot of water. This will help to control your hunger levels and regulate your body's systems while you're adjusting to your new diet.

Exercise, fasting, and supplements can also be helpful in keeping you feeling full and focused as you achieve a ketogenic state. You can learn more about these practices elsewhere in the guide.

How do I know if my body is in ketosis?

There are both urine and blood strips available on the market to test if your body is in ketosis. (Though there is a lot of debate over whether they are worth the purchase.) You could drive yourself crazy measuring and testing your body's ketone levels. But, it's much easier to check for the hallmark symptoms of ketosis to ensure your body is still on track.

If you find yourself going to the bathroom frequently during the early stages that's a good sign. Look for increased urination, since the keto diet is a natural diuretic. The more you have to go to the bathroom, the more likely your body is entering a ketogenic state.

In addition, you may find yourself experiencing dry mouth. The more you urinate, the thirstier you will become and the drier your mouth will be. In order to avoid dry mouth, you should remember to drink plenty of water and get additional electrolytes like sodium, potassium, and magnesium from your food sources.

Bad breath is another sign of ketosis. Acetone in your body is a ketone that can be excreted into your breath. When this happens, it can make your breath smell like nail polish remover. Fortunately, this symptom isn't long-lasting and should go away as your body maintains its ketogenic state.

The final sign that your body is in ketosis is that you have reduced hunger levels while having more energy. Once you get past your initial "keto flu" symptoms, you will find yourself feeling much clearer mentally and full of healthy energy.

Do I really need to count calories?

At the end of the day, weight loss comes down to calories in versus calories out, and how well your hormones work for your metabolism. In order to drop down a pant size, you have to know that you are creating a calorie deficit.

Fortunately, by keeping track of your protein, carb, and fat intake, you are also taking into account the amount of calories you are eating.

But, if you exercise a lot in a given day, you may want to watch your calorie count to ensure you aren't creating too much of deficit and eating into your muscle mass.

Can I have too much fat?

You absolutely can eat too much fat on the keto diet. If you want to lose weight, you need to closely monitor your fat intake. Make sure that you aren't creating a calorie surplus.

If you find that you aren't losing much weight on the keto diet, your first defense is to look at the amount of fat you are consuming.

How much weight can I lose on the keto diet?

The amount of weight you shed during your keto diet is completely dependent on your choices. The more you restrict your carbs, and the more exercise you add to your routine, the more fat loss you will see.

You can also pad your progress by cutting out common triggers for diet failure. If you want to be successful long-term, consider cutting out artificial sweeteners, seed oils, dairy, wheat, and wheat byproducts before you start the diet.

Make sure you stick with your keto diet for at least a couple of months if you want to see consistent weight loss. A lot of the weight you will lose during your first few days on the diet will be water weight due to its diuretic effect on your body. A lot of those first few pounds will be pure water weight and little to no fat loss, so keep on going.

I just started and feel terrible, should I keep going?

When you first start the keto diet, it's common to suffer from the "keto flu," which is a series of flu-like symptoms. That doesn't mean you should give up right away and go back to a carb-rich diet.

Try to stick with the diet and drink lots of water with electrolytes while your body adjusts. If you don't feel better after a week or two, the diet may need to be modified to accommodate your needs. Remember, there are a wide variety of keto diets out there all designed by people who felt their needs would be better met with a slight change in the design. Don't be afraid to customize the diet to make it work for you.

Optimally, this will be the last "diet" you ever go on because it will really feel more like a lifestyle change. The changes you make should be easy to adhere to, make your body feel better, and result in the health goals you're looking to achieve.

I'm constipated, can you help?

It's common for new keto dieters to feel constipated. Fortunately, there is a lot you can do to get your bowels going again.

Consider taking a magnesium supplement, along with a big glass of water. You may also want to try eating a tablespoon of coconut oil and more fibrous vegetables. If you don't have enough dietary fiber in your digestive system, it's difficult for your body to keep things moving.

I like to work out. Is the keto diet right for me?

If you like to perform a lot of cardio, like going on regular runs, swimming, or biking, you will find yourself feeling healthy and satisfied on the keto diet. Just make sure you monitor your protein intake so that your body can sustain its muscle mass as you train.

If you like to lift weights, you need to focus on your protein even more. You may also want to add in some additional carbohydrates after major lifting sessions to help your body rebuild after a heavy workout.

What is a keto bomb and should I make one?

A keto bomb is a drink, often coffee or tea, that is loaded with fat from a source like oil or butter. They're common for people on the keto diet who are worried about getting enough calories and maintaining their energy levels. They also can be used to curb hunger in between meals.

Keto bombs are generally not necessary for people on the diet who manage their diets well and eat a lot of fatty meat and fish. If you add keto bombs to your diet, you risk overconsuming your allotted amount of fat for the day.

If you are using the keto diet to lose weight, then avoid keto bombs for now. Once you have hit your target weight goal, they may be just what you need to maintain your optimal weight level.

Part Two: The 7-Day Meal Plan

I've made it easy for you to get started on the keto diet with this 7-day meal plan. It includes recipes from this book, so there's no need to spend time searching the Internet. Each day includes the daily totals for calories, fat, protein, and net carbs to keep you on track. The meal plan is based on a daily intake of 1,200 – 1,400 calories, which is optimal for losing weight. If you need to increase your caloric intake, you can add a midmorning snack, or just eat a larger portion of your favorite recipes.

Monday
Breakfast: Ham & Asparagus Frittata
Lunch: Cheesesteak Wraps
Snack: Spicy Glazed Pecans
Dinner: Broccoli & Cheese Stuffed Chicken
Per Day
Calories 1,308 / Fat 97
Protein 35/ Net Carbs 19

Tuesday
Breakfast: Sausage Hand Pies
Lunch: Chili Verde
Snack: Cajun Portobello Chips
Dinner: Beef with Basil Sauce & Basic Cauliflower Rice
Per Day
Calories 1,259 / Fat 83
Protein 95 / Net Carbs 28

Wednesday
Breakfast: Blackberry Cheesecake Smoothie
Lunch: Bacon & Beer Braised Cabbage
Snack: Basil & Cheese Crackers
Dinner: Asparagus and Salmon
Per Day
Calories 1,535 / Fat 121
Protein 74 / Net Carbs 24

Thursday
Breakfast: Green Chili Quiche
Lunch: Creamy Clam Chowder
Snack: Barbecued Almonds
Dinner: Beef & Blue Cheese Casserole
Per Day
Calories 1,358 / Fat 100
Protein 90 / Net Carbs 21

Friday
Breakfast: Raspberry Cinnamon Smoothie
Lunch: Parmesan Cod Nuggets and Fried Green Beans
Snack: Hot Cauliflower Bites
Dinner: Chicken, Cheese & Mushroom Casserole
Per Day
Calories 1,422 / Fat 91
Protein 103 / Net Carbs 21

Saturday
Breakfast: Breakfast Stuffed Bell Peppers
Lunch: Southern Spicy Chicken & Cheesy Cauliflower Mash
Snack: Zucchini Pizza Bites
Dinner: Cajun Salmon & Creamy Baked Squash
Per Day
Calories 1,341 / Fat 96
Protein 128 / Net Carbs 31

Sunday
Breakfast: Almond Crusted Bagels
Lunch: Crab Mac 'N' Cheese
Snack: Onion Cheese Dip
Dinner: Beef Brisket with Carrots & Onions
Per Day
Calories 1,181 / Fat 83
Protein 90 / Net Carbs 14

Week One Shopping List

Produce
4 lbs. broccoli
2 large heads of garlic
2 lbs. mushrooms
2 lbs. portobello mushrooms
10 oz. bag of fresh spinach
2 lbs. summer squash
2 zucchini
2 jalapeno peppers
1 head Savoy cabbage
1 head of lettuce
1 ½ lbs. green beans
3 carrots
9 lbs. cauliflower
1 lb. Brussel Sprouts
8 green bell peppers
3 red bell peppers
1 lb. asparagus
1 bunch of celery
1 bunch of green onions
2 shallots
9 onions
Fresh herbs:
Parsley
Cilantro
Basil (x2)
Thyme
Rosemary
1 pint of blackberries

2 lemons
1 lime

Dairy
7 cups mozzarella cheese
5 cups sharp cheddar cheese
3 oz. soft goat cheese
4 pkgs. cream cheese
2 cups cheddar Jack cheese
1 cup Mexican-blend cheese
1 cup Swiss cheese
5 oz. blue cheese
1 ½ cups Monterey Jack Cheese
½ cup provolone cheese
3 dozen eggs
½ gallon unsweetened almond milk
1 quart half-and-half
8 oz. sour cream
1 quart heavy cream
1 lb. butter

Misc
2 large cans of diced green chilies
6 cups pecan halves
2 ¼ cups raw almonds
1 large container Parmesan cheese
1 jar marinara sauce
I bottle blonde beer
1 bag frozen raspberries

Meat & Seafood
2 pkgs. bacon
1 lb. breakfast sausage
¼ lb. ham
2 lbs. ground beef
1 lb. sirloin steak
4-5 lb. beef brisket
4 lbs. boneless, skinless chicken breasts
2 lb. boneless pork shoulder
1 lb. medium shrimp
4 salmon fillets
1 lb. cod
3 oz. lump crab meat
18 oz. clams

Part Three: The Recipes

Breakfast & Smoothies

Almond Crusted Bagels

Serves: 8 / Prep time: 20 minutes / Cook time: 10 minutes

Who says you can't enjoy bagels while on the keto diet? These almond crusted bagels hit the spot when you are craving something slightly sweet, and they are gluten-free.

Ingredients:
3 eggs, divided
3 cups mozzarella cheese, grated
1 ¾ cups almond flour, sifted
¼ cup almonds, chopped fine
2 oz. cream cheese, soft
1 tbsp. baking powder

Instructions
1. Preheat oven to 400 degrees. Lightly spray a baking sheet with cooking spray.
2. In a small bowl, sift together flour and baking powder. Set aside.
3. Place the mozzarella and cream cheese in a large, microwave safe bowl. Microwave on high for 30-second intervals, stirring each time, until cheese is completely melted.
4. Affix the dough blade attachment to your food processor. Add the melted cheese, flour mixture, and 2 eggs. Process on high until ingredients are combined and form a sticky dough.
5. Cover a cutting board with plastic wrap, running the wrap completely around the board to keep it taut. Place dough on board and divide into 8 equal pieces. If dough is too sticky, lightly oil your hands to make it easier to work with.
6. Form each piece into ropes that are 1-inch thick. Form the ropes into a circle and pinch the ends together. Place on the prepared pan.
7. In a small bowl, beat remaining egg. Brush the tops of the bagels with the egg, then sprinkle 1 tablespoon nuts over the top.
8. Bake 10-12 minutes until bagels are golden brown and have puffed up. Serve.

Nutrition Facts Per Serving
Calories 177 / Fat 14g / Protein 9g / Carbs 5g / Fiber 2g / Net Carbs 3g

Blackberry Cheesecake Smoothie

Serves: 1 / Prep time: 5 minutes / Cook time: 5 minutes

Who says you can't have cheesecake for breakfast? This blackberry smoothie delivers all the great flavors of your favorite cheesecake without all the carbs.

Ingredients:
1 cup unsweetened almond milk
3/4 cup blackberries
7 tbsp. cream cheese
1 tbsp. coconut oil
1 tsp. stevia
½ tsp. vanilla

Instructions
1. Place all ingredients in a blender and process until smooth and combined. Pour into a chilled glass and enjoy.

Nutrition Facts Per Serving
Calories 454 / Fat 42g / Protein 8g / Carbs 14g / Fiber 7g / Net Carbs 7g

Breakfast Stuffed Bell Peppers

Serves: 4 / Prep time: 10 minutes / Cook time: 6 hours

Stuffed bell peppers aren't just for dinner anymore. Try stuffing them with your favorite breakfast ingredients, then slow cook them to perfection.

Ingredients:
6 eggs
4 bell peppers, seeds & ribs removed
½ lb. breakfast sausage
½ cup cheddar Jack cheese, grated
½ cup water
4 oz. green chilies, diced
2 tbsp. green onion, diced
¼ tsp. salt
1/8 tsp. pepper

Instructions
1. Place a skillet over medium-high heat. Add sausage and cook, breaking up with a spoon, until no longer pink. Transfer to a bowl and drain off fat.
2. Place the peppers in a crock pot and pour the water around them.
3. In a medium bowl, whisk eggs until smooth. Stir in sausage, cheese, chilies, salt, and pepper until combined. Fill the peppers with the egg mixture.
5. Add the lid and cook on high for 4 hours. Peppers are done when the eggs are set. Garnish with green onions and serve.

Nutrition Facts Per Serving
Calories 364 / Fat 22g / Protein 27g / Carbs 15g / Fiber 2g / Net Carbs 13g

Green Chili Quiche

Serves: 6 / Prep time: 5 minutes / Cook time: 30 minutes

A spicy breakfast quiche without the crust. This easy breakfast is also gluten-free and vegetarian-friendly.

Ingredients:
6 eggs
1 cup half-and-half
1 cup Mexican-blend cheese, grated
¼ cup cilantro, chopped
10 oz. green chilies, diced
½ tsp. salt
½ tsp. cumin

Instructions
1. Preheat oven to 350 degrees. Spray an 8-inch baking dish with cooking spray.
2. In a large bowl, beat eggs, then stir in half-and-half, chilies, salt, cumin, and half of the cheese.
3. Pour into prepared baking dish and cover with foil.
4. Bake 20 minutes. Remove the foil and sprinkle with remaining cheese.
5. Bake another 8-10 minutes until eggs are set and cheese is melted and lightly browned. Let cool 5 minutes before slicing. Serve garnished with cilantro.

Nutrition Facts Per Serving
Calories 202 / Fat 16g / Protein 11g / Carbs 4g / Fiber 0g / Net Carbs 4g

Ham & Asparagus Frittata

Serves: 6 / Prep time: 10 minutes / Cook time: 30 minutes

A tasty, healthy breakfast that is perfect for busy mornings. Ham, asparagus, eggs, and cheese all come together in a quick-to-prepare casserole.

Ingredients:
6 eggs
2 cups asparagus, chopped
1 cup ham, cubed
1 cup red bell pepper, seeded & sliced
1 cup half-and-half
1 cup cheddar cheese, grated
1 tbsp. butter, soft
2 tsp. black pepper
1 tsp. salt

Instructions
1. Preheat oven to 350 degrees. Grease an 8-inch baking dish with the softened butter.
2. Place the peppers in an even layer at the bottom of the dish. Top with ham, then asparagus.
3. In a large bowl, whisk together eggs, half-and-half, salt, and pepper.
4. Stir in cheese and pour mixture over ingredients in the baking dish. Cover with foil.
5. Bake 20 minutes, then remove the foil and bake another 5-10 minutes, until eggs are set and top is lightly browned. Let cool 5 minutes before slicing and serving.

Nutrition Facts Per Serving
Calories 262 / Fat 19g / Protein 16g / Carbs 7g / Fiber 2g / Net Carbs 5g

Raspberry Cinnamon Smoothie

Serves: 1 / Prep time: 5 minutes / Cook time: 5 minutes

The cinnamon helps bring out the flavor of the raspberries, while the addition of spinach adds a healthy dose of vitamins to this breakfast smoothie.

Ingredients:
1 cup unsweetened almond milk
1 cup fresh spinach
½ cup frozen raspberries
2 tbsp. almond butter
¼ tsp. cinnamon

Instructions
1. Place all ingredients in a blender and process until smooth. Pour into a chilled glass and enjoy.

Nutrition Facts Per Serving
Calories 286 / Fat 21g / Protein 10g / Carbs 19g / Fiber 10g / Net Carbs 9g

Sausage Hand Pies

Serves: 4 / Prep time: 10 minutes / Cook time: 20 minutes

A handy all-in-one breakfast treat that you can take on the go. Eggs and sausage wrapped up in a cheesy, crisp dough—all the flavor without the carbs.

Ingredients:
4 sausage patties, cooked & chopped
4 eggs, beaten
1 ½ cup mozzarella cheese, grated
2/3 cup almond flour, sifted
4 tbsp. butter

Instructions
1. Preheat oven to 400 degrees. Lightly spray a baking sheet with cooking spray.
2. In a microwave safe bowl, melt the mozzarella cheese until smooth.
3. Stir in flour until thoroughly combined.
4. Roll the dough out between 2 sheets of parchment paper. Use a sharp knife to cut dough into 4 equal rectangles.
5. Heat the butter in a skillet over medium heat. Add the eggs and scramble to desired doneness.
6. Divide eggs evenly between the four pieces of dough, placing them on one side. Top with sausage pieces.
7. Fold dough over filling and seal the edges with a fork. Poke a few holes on the top of the pies.
8. Place the pies on the baking sheet and bake 20 minutes or until golden brown. Serve immediately.

Nutrition Facts Per Serving
Calories 371 / Fat 30g / Protein 21g / Carbs 8g / Fiber 2g / Net Carbs 6g

Spinach Baked Eggs

Serves: 4 / Prep time: 5 minutes / Cook time: 20 minutes

A light, healthy breakfast that will fuel your body and get you through a busy morning. These baked eggs in spinach are gluten-free and vegetarian-friendly.

Ingredients:
4 eggs
1 tomato, diced fine
4 cups baby spinach
½ cup Parmesan cheese, grated
2 cloves garlic, diced fine
2 tsp. olive oil

Instructions
1. Preheat the oven to 350 degrees. Lightly coat an 8x8-inch baking dish with cooking spray.
2. Heat the oil in a large skillet over medium heat. Add the spinach and garlic and cook, stirring occasionally, until spinach has wilted, about 2 minutes. Drain off excess liquid.
3. Stir in Parmesan and transfer to prepared baking dish. Make 4 small indents in the spinach and crack an egg in each one.
4. Bake 15-20 minutes, or until egg whites are cooked and yolks are still slightly runny.
5. Let cool 5 minutes. Serve topped with tomatoes.

Nutrition Facts Per Serving
Calories 139 / Fat 10g / Protein 12g / Carbs 3g / Fiber 1g / Net Carbs 2g

Appetizers & Snacks

Basil & Cheese Crackers

Serves: 4 / Prep time: 15 minutes / Cook time: 10 minutes

When you are craving something salty and crunchy grab a handful of these tasty crackers. You can substitute the basil for any other herb, like rosemary or oregano, and they will be just as good.

Ingredients:
1 cup cheddar cheese, coarsely grated
¼ cup Parmesan cheese, grated
¼ cup coconut flour
6 tbsp. butter, softened
2 tbsp. heavy cream
2 tbsp. fresh basil, coarsely chopped

Instructions
1. Preheat oven to 325 degrees. Line a baking sheet with parchment paper.
2. In a medium bowl, beat together butter and cream until smooth.
3. Add the cheddar and Parmesan cheeses and mix well. Stir in the flour.
4. Use your hands to incorporate the basil and form a smooth dough. Form the dough into a ball.
5. Line a work surface with parchment paper and place the dough in the middle. Top with a second piece of parchment paper and roll dough to ¼-inch thick. Use a small cookie cutter to cut out shapes. Carefully transfer cut-out shapes to prepared pan. Reroll dough and repeat until all the dough is used.
6. Bake 12 minutes, or until crackers are golden brown. Remove to a wire rack to cool. Repeat with any remaining dough. Store the crackers in an airtight container until ready to serve.

Nutrition Facts Per Serving
Calories 380 / Fat 35g / Protein 15g / Carbs 2g / Fiber 0g / Net Carbs 2g

Barbecued Almonds

Serves: 8 / Prep time: 5 minutes / Cook time: 45 minutes

A tasty snack that you will want to keep on hand. This treat will satisfy that craving for something crunchy and salty. Plus, unlike the store-bought variety, you will know exactly what ingredients are used to make them.

Ingredients:
2 cups raw almonds, soaked in water overnight
1 tbsp. olive oil
1 tbsp. paprika
2 tsp. salt
2 tsp. chili powder
1 tsp. garlic powder
1 tsp. onion powder
1 tsp. cumin
1 tsp. black pepper

Instructions:
1. Preheat oven to 300 degrees. Line a baking sheet with parchment paper.
2. Drain almonds and place on paper towels, pat dry.
3. In a small bowl, combine the spices and mix well
4. Place almonds in large mixing bowl and add oil and spices. Toss to coat well.
5. Spread in a single layer on prepared pan and bake 45 minutes. Stir occasionally. If almonds are not crunchy after 45 minutes, continue baking until they reach desired consistency.
6. Remove from oven and let cool. Store in airtight container.

Nutrition Facts Per Serving
Calories 161 / Fat 14g / Protein 5g / Carbs 5g / Fiber 4g / Net Carbs 1g

Cajun Portobello Chips

Serves: 4 / Prep time: 10 minutes / Cook time: 1 hour

Potassium tends to be lacking in most low-carb diets. These flavorful mushroom chips give you a boost of potassium while satisfying the need to snack.

Ingredients:
5 cups portobello mushrooms, sliced thin
4 tbsp. coconut oil, melted
1 tbsp. Cajun seasoning, or to taste
½ tsp. salt
¼ tsp. black pepper

Instructions
1. Preheat oven to 300 degrees. Line a baking sheet with parchment paper.
2. In a small bowl, combine the seasonings and mix well.
3. Place the mushrooms in a single layer on prepared pan. Brush with melted oil and sprinkle with seasonings.
4. Bake 45-60 minutes until golden brown and crispy, stirring occasionally. Serve warm.

Nutrition Facts Per Serving
Calories 169 / Fat 15g / Protein 3g / Carbs 4g / Fiber 1g / Net Carbs 3g

Hot Cauliflower Bites

Serves: 4 / Prep time: 5 minutes / Cook time: 20 minutes

All the flavor of Buffalo wings without all the fat and calories. Perfect for an afternoon snack or while watching your favorite game on TV.

Ingredients:
1 large head of cauliflower, separated into small florets
2/3 cup wing sauce
3 tbsp. olive oil
2 tbsp. butter, melted
1 tsp. garlic salt
1/8 tsp. pepper

Instructions:
1. Preheat oven to 450 degrees.
2. In a medium bowl, add cauliflower and drizzle with oil. Toss to coat. Add garlic salt and pepper. Again, toss to coat evenly.
3. Place on an ungreased baking sheet. Bake 15 minutes, turning florets once after 5 minutes. Check after 10 minutes for desired doneness.
4. Melt butter in a glass bowl in the microwave. Add wing sauce to butter and whisk to combine.
5. Remove cauliflower from oven and toss them in the hot sauce to coat evenly.
6. Return them to the pan and bake another 5 minutes.
7. Serve with ranch or blue cheese dressing for dipping.

Nutrition Facts Per Serving
Calories 190 / Fat 16g / Protein 4g / Carbs 4g / Fiber 1g / Net Carbs 3g

Mushrooms Stuffed with Bacon & Cheese

Serves: 4 / Prep time: 10 minutes / Cook time: 25 minutes

Mushroom caps stuffed with bacon, chives, and plenty of cheese - delicious! Serve these at your next party to impress your guests.

Ingredients:
12 mushrooms, rinsed & stems removed
8 oz. bacon
7 oz. cream cheese, soft
3 tbsp. fresh chives, chopped fine
2 tbsp. butter, soft
1 tsp. paprika
Salt & pepper, to taste

Instructions
1. Preheat oven to 400 degrees. Lightly coat a baking sheet with cooking spray.
2. In a large skillet, over medium-high heat, cook bacon until crisp. Transfer to paper towel-lined plate to cool.
3. Chop the mushroom stems and add them to the bacon fat. Cook, stirring occasionally for 3-5 minutes, until tender.
4. Lay the mushroom caps on the prepared pan, top sides down.
5. In a large bowl, crumble the bacon and add the fried mushroom pieces. Stir in remaining ingredients.
6. Spoon the bacon mixture into each mushroom cap. Bake 20 minutes, or until mushrooms are golden brown. Serve warm.

Nutrition Facts Per Serving
Calories 341 / Fat 37g / Protein 13g / Carbs 4g / Fiber 1g / Net Carbs 3g

Onion Cheese Dip

Serves: 8 / Prep time: 10 minutes / Cook time: 40 minutes

This cheesy onion dip is great for game-day snacking. Serve it with your favorite raw vegetables, like carrot sticks or celery, for a healthy snack.

Ingredients:
1 cup Swiss cheese, grated
1 cup mayonnaise
1 cup onion, grated
8 oz. cream cheese, soft

Instructions
1. Preheat oven to 350 degrees.
2. In a medium bowl, combine all ingredients and mix thoroughly. Transfer to a small baking dish and cover tightly with foil.
3. Bake 30 minutes. Remove the foil and stir well. Bake another 5-10 minutes until dip is hot and top is starting to brown. Serve.

Nutrition Facts Per Serving
Calories 352 / Fat 35g / Protein 6g / Carbs 3g / Fiber 0g / Net Carbs 3g

Spicy Glazed Pecans

Serves: 12 / Prep time: 5 minutes / Cook time: 30 minutes

These spicy glazed nuts will wake up your taste buds and keep you going until dinnertime. If you don't like a lot of spice, just reduce the amounts of hot sauce and curry powder.

Ingredients:
6 cups pecan halves
¼ cup Worcestershire sauce
6 tbsp. butter, melted
2 tbsp. hot sauce
1 tbsp. soy sauce
1 tbsp. hot curry powder
1 tbsp. chili powder

Instructions
1. Preheat oven to 275 degrees. Lightly coat a baking sheet with cooking spray.
2. In a large bowl, combine all ingredients and toss well to coat the pecans. Spread out on the prepared pan.
3. Bake 20 minutes, stirring at the halfway point. Dump contents onto a parchment-lined baking sheet and spread out to cool. Serve warm, or at room temperature. Store in an airtight container.

Nutrition Facts Per Serving
Calories 402 / Fat 41g / Protein 5g / Carbs 9g / Fiber 5g / Net Carbs 4g

Zucchini Pizza Bites

Serves: 6 / Prep time: 10 minutes / Cook time: 10 minutes

Satisfy your craving for pizza with this healthy alternative. Sliced zucchini is topped with your favorite pizza ingredients for a tasty snack.

Ingredients:
2 zucchini, cut in ¼-inch slices
1/3 cup mini pepperoni
¼ cup marinara sauce, sugar-free
¼ cup mozzarella cheese, grated
¼ cup parmesan cheese, grated
2 tbsp. olive oil
2 tbsp. Italian seasoning
1 tsp. salt
1 tsp. pepper

Instructions
1. Preheat oven to 400 degrees. Line a baking sheet with parchment paper.
2. Lay the zucchini, in a single layer, on the parchment. Brush with oil and sprinkle with Italian seasoning, salt, and pepper.
4. Top each slice of zucchini with marinara, both cheeses, and pepperoni.
5. Bake 10 minutes, or until cheese is melted and bubbly. Serve warm.

Nutrition Facts Per Serving
Calories 142 / Fat 11g / Protein 7g / Carbs 4g / Fiber 1g / Net Carbs 6g

Meats & Poultry

Bacon & Beer Braised Cabbage

Serves: 4 / Prep time: 5 minutes / Cook time: 15 minutes

Cabbage cooked in beer and topped with crispy bacon—yes, please! This tasty dinner can be ready and on the table in less than 30 minutes, making it perfect for a week-night meal.

Ingredients:
1 Savoy cabbage, sliced in strips
1 onion, sliced in strips
3 ½ oz. bacon, chopped
1 cup blonde beer
1 tbsp. butter

Instructions
1. Melt the butter in a large, deep skillet over medium heat.
2. Add onion and bacon and cook, stirring occasionally, until onion is soft, about 5 minutes.
3. Add the cabbage and beer, stir to mix well.
4. Cook, stirring occasionally, until cabbage is tender, about 10 minutes. Serve immediately.

Nutrition Facts Per Serving
Calories 267 / Fat 18g / Protein 9g / Carbs 15g / Fiber 6g / Net Carbs 9g

Beef & Blue Cheese Casserole

Serves: 4 / Prep time: 5 minutes / Cook time: 20 minutes

A new twist on the usual ground beef casserole. Green beans and blue cheese add new flavors and it is quick to prepare.

Ingredients:
1 lb. ground beef
1 onion, chopped fine
1 cup fresh green beans, trimmed and cut into bite-size pieces
1 cup heavy cream
½ cup cheddar cheese, grated
¼ cup butter
5 oz. blue cheese
Salt & pepper, to taste

Instructions
1. Preheat oven to 400 degrees.
2. Melt butter in a large skillet over medium-high heat. Add ground beef and onions and cook until beef is no longer pink.
3. Add the beans and blue cheese and stir to mix well.
4. Stir in the cream and bring to a simmer. Season with salt and pepper to taste.
5. Transfer mixture to an 8-inch baking dish and sprinkle cheese on top.
6. Bake 15-20 minutes, until golden brown.

Nutrition Facts Per Serving
Calories 618 / Fat 46g / Protein 47g / Carbs 6g / Fiber 2g / Net Carbs 4g

Beef Brisket with Carrots & Onions

Serves: 10 / Prep time: 35 minutes / Cook time: 8 hours

Bring back those Sunday roast beef dinners. This meal is slow-cooked in the crock pot all day. Just add the ingredients in the morning, then spend the day how you like. Dinner is ready when you are.

Ingredients:
4 -5 lb. beef brisket
6 cloves garlic, chopped fine
4 bay leaves
3 onions, sliced
3 carrots, peeled & sliced ½-inch thick
1 sprig thyme
1 sprig rosemary
2 cups beef broth, low sodium
2 tbsp. olive oil
1 tbsp. mustard
1 ½ tsp. salt

Instructions
1. Use a sharp knife to score the fat side of the brisket in parallel lines, being careful to only slice through the fat, not the meat. Repeat to create a cross-hatch pattern. Sprinkle with salt and let sit 30 minutes.
2. Heat the oil in a large skillet over medium-high heat. Add the brisket, fat side down, and cook 5-8 minutes to render the fat. Turn meat over and cook until browned on the other side. Transfer to the crock pot.
3. Add the onions to the skillet and season with salt. Cook, stirring frequently, until onions are browned, about 5-8 minutes. Add the garlic and cook 1 minute more. Add to the beef.
4. Add the carrots, bay leaves, thyme, and rosemary to the crock pot. Whisk the broth and mustard together until smooth and pour over ingredients in the crock pot.
5. Cover with the lid and cook on low heat 8-9 hours, or until brisket is tender. Transfer meat to a cutting board and tent with foil to keep warm. Let rest 10-15 minutes, then slice across the grain. Serve with the cooked carrots and onions and some of the cooking liquid.

Nutrition Facts Per Serving
Calories 398 / Fat 15g / Protein 56g / Carbs 6g / Fiber 1g / Net Carbs 5g

Beef with Basil Sauce

Serves: 4 / Prep time: 5 minutes / Cook time: 15 minutes

This is an easy, Asian-inspired dinner to make after a long day. The rich sauce goes well with cauliflower rice or our keto-friendly noodles (see Side Dishes).

Ingredients:
7 cloves garlic, sliced
2 shallots, sliced thin
1/2 red bell pepper, sliced thin
1 lb. lean ground beef
1 cup basil leaves, chopped
½ cup beef broth, low sodium
¼ cup water
6 tbsp. soy sauce, low sodium
2 tbsp. olive oil
2 tbsp. fish sauce
1 tbsp. fresh ginger, peeled & grated
3 tsp. oyster sauce
2 tsp. brown sugar
1 tsp. cornstarch

Instructions
1. Heat oil in a large skillet over medium-high heat.
2. Add the shallots, garlic, ginger, and bell peppers to the pan and cook, stirring frequently, for 3 minutes. Use a slotted spoon to transfer mixture to a bowl.
3. Increase heat to high and add the ground beef. Cook, breaking it up with a spoon, until beef is no longer pink.
4. In a small bowl, whisk together brown sugar, fish sauce, soy sauce, oyster sauce, cornstarch, broth, and water until smooth.
5. Add the pepper mixture back to the pan and pour the sauce over. Cook, stirring for 2 minutes, until sauce has thickened.
6. Stir in basil and cook until wilted, about 2 minutes. Serve over hot cauliflower rice.

Nutrition Facts Per Serving
Calories 359 / Fat 20g / Protein 34g / Carbs 10g / Fiber 1g / Net Carbs 9g

Broccoli & Cheese Stuffed Chicken

Serves: 4 / Prep time: 15 minutes / Cook time: 25 minutes

These cheesy chicken breasts are a great way to get the kids to eat their vegetables. They are ideal when you want to whip up something quick and tasty for dinner.

Ingredients:
1 lb. chicken breasts, boneless & skinless
1 ¼ cups broccoli, cooked & drained
1 ¼ cups Colby-Jack cheese, grated
¾ cup bell pepper, diced
1 tbsp. olive oil
1 tbsp. mayonnaise
1 ½ tsp. garlic powder, divided
¾ tsp. onion powder
½ tsp. paprika
¼ tsp. salt
¼ tsp. pepper

Instructions:
1. Preheat the oven to 400 degrees. Use the oil to grease an 8-inch baking dish.
2. Place chicken on a cutting board and cut a pocket; make sure not to cut all the way through.
3. In a large bowl, combine broccoli, bell pepper, cheese, mayonnaise, and ½ tsp. garlic powder. Mix well.
4. Stuff the chicken with the broccoli mixture.
5. In a small bowl, stir together onion powder, 1 tsp. garlic powder, pepper, salt, and paprika. Sprinkle both sides of the chicken with the mixture and place in prepared dish.
6. Bake 20-25 minutes, flipping halfway through, until chicken is cooked through and golden brown. Serve immediately.

Nutrition Facts Per Serving
Calories 325 / Fat 18g / Protein 35g / Carbs 7g / Fiber 1g / Net Carbs 6g

Cheesesteak Wraps

Serves: 4 / Prep time: 10 minutes / Cook time: 10 minutes

You don't have to give up all your favorite foods to stick to the keto diet. With some small tweaks, you can even eat cheesesteaks.

Ingredients:
8 large lettuce leaves
1 onion, sliced in strips
1 green bell pepper, sliced in strips
1 red bell pepper, sliced in strips
1 lb. lean sirloin steak, sliced in very thin strips
½ cup provolone cheese, grated
2 tbsp. cilantro, chopped
½ tbsp. olive oil
2 tsp. oregano
½ tsp. salt
¼ tsp. pepper

Instructions
1. Heat oil in a large skillet over medium-high heat.
2. Season steak with salt and pepper and add to the skillet, along with the oregano, onion, and bell peppers. Cook, stirring frequently for 5-10, minutes until beef is cooked and vegetables are tender.
3. Place 2 lettuce leaves on each serving plate. Spoon beef mixture onto lettuce and top with cheese and cilantro. Serve.

Nutrition Facts Per Serving
Calories 319 / Fat 19g / Protein 29g / Carbs 7g / Fiber 3g / Net Carbs 4g

Chicken, Cheese & Mushroom Casserole

Serves: 6 / Prep time: 10 minutes / Cook time: 30 minutes

This easy chicken casserole will quickly become one of your favorite go-to dinners. You can have this on the table in less than an hour, making it perfect for those hectic week nights.

Ingredients:
1 lb. mushrooms, sliced
1 lb. cauliflower, cooked & drained
2 stalks celery, chopped fine
3 cups chicken, cooked & shredded
8 oz. cream cheese, soft
8 oz. Monterey Jack cheese, grated
1 tbsp. butter
1 tbsp. dried onion, chopped
½ tsp. salt
½ tsp. pepper

Instructions
1. Preheat oven to 350 degrees. Spray a 2-quart casserole dish with cooking spray.
2. Melt butter in a skillet over medium heat. Add celery, onion, and mushrooms and cook 3-4 minutes, or until vegetables start to soften.
3. Stir in cream cheese until blended. Then stir in the chicken.
4. Chop the cauliflower and add it, along with remaining ingredients, stir to combine. Transfer mixture to prepared casserole dish and cover with foil.
5. Bake 20-25 minutes. Remove foil and bake another 10 minutes, or until top is golden brown and casserole is bubbly. Serve immediately.

Nutrition Facts Per Serving
Calories 386 / Fat 23g / Protein 38g / Carbs 8g / Fiber 3g / Net Carbs 5g

Chili Verde

Serves: 6 / Prep time: 15 minutes / Cook time: 8 hours

This chili verde is the perfect meal to warm you up on those cold winter days. Tender bites of pork mixed with green chilies and bell peppers with just a hint of lime.

Ingredients:
3 cloves garlic, chopped fine
2 green bell peppers, cut in 1-inch pieces
2 jalapeño peppers, seeded & chopped
2 lbs. pork shoulder, boneless & cut in 1-inch pieces
2 cups chicken broth, low-sodium
1 ½ cups onion, chopped
½ cup cilantro, chopped
1/3 cup sour cream
4 ½ oz. green chilies, diced & undrained
3 tbsp. olive oil, divided
2 tbsp. flour
2 tbsp. lime juice
1 ½ tsp. cumin
1 tsp. chili powder
1 tsp. salt
¾ tsp. oregano

Instructions
1. In a large bowl, stir together flour and salt. Add the pork and toss to coat.
2. Heat 2 tbsp. oil in a large skillet on medium-high heat. Add the pork, in batches, and cook until browned on all sides. Transfer to crock pot.
3. Reduce heat to medium and add remaining oil. Add the onion, bell peppers, jalapeños, and oregano and cook 2 minutes, stirring occasionally.
4. Add garlic, cumin, and chili powder and cook, stirring, 1 minute. Stir in broth, green chilies, and half the cilantro, mix well. Pour over pork.
5. Cover with the lid and cook on low heat 6-8 hours, until pork is tender.
6. Stir in the lime juice and remaining cilantro. Serve topped with a dollop of sour cream.

Nutrition Facts Per Serving
Calories 312 / Fat 14g / Protein 36g / Carbs 10g / Fiber 2g / Net Carbs 8g

Mustard Crusted Pork Chops

Serves: 2 / Prep time: 5 minutes / Cook time: 15 minutes

A delicious new way to season pork chops. Replace the usual bread crumbs with crushed pork rinds and enjoy a crispy coating on any fried food.

Ingredients:
2 pork chops, 1-inch thick
1 cup pork rinds, crushed
¼ cup spicy brown mustard
3 tbsp. olive oil
½ tsp. salt
½ tsp. pepper
½ tsp. oregano
½ tsp. garlic powder
½ tsp. parsley
¼ tsp. basil
¼ tsp. onion powder

Instructions
1. In a small bowl, combine pork rinds and seasonings and transfer to a shallow dish.
2. Spread mustard on both sides of the pork chops. Dip in pork rind mixture, pressing to coat.
3. Heat oil in a large skillet over medium heat. Add pork chops and cook 12-15 minutes, until nicely browned on the outside, flipping them over halfway through cooking time. Serve.

Nutrition Facts Per Serving
Calories 542 / Fat 30g / Protein 36g / Carbs 1g / Fiber 1g / Net Carbs 0g

Southern Spicy Chicken

Serves: 4 / Prep time: 5 minutes / Cook time: 20 minutes

Down South they like it hot and this chicken recipe is a great example of that. You can tone down the heat by eliminating the cayenne pepper if you like.

Ingredients:
2 lbs. chicken breasts, boneless & skinless
3 tbsp. olive oil
2 tsp. paprika
1 tsp. salt
1 tsp. onion powder
1 tsp. garlic powder
1 tsp. oregano
1 tsp. pepper
1 tsp. thyme
½ tsp. cayenne pepper

Instructions
1. In a medium bowl, combine the spices and seasonings and mix well.
2. Coat all sides of the chicken with the spice mixture.
3. Heat oil in a large skillet over medium-high heat. Add the chicken and brown it, 3-5 minutes per side. Reduce heat and cook until chicken is no longer pink in the middle, about 8-10 minutes. Serve.

Nutrition Facts Per Serving
Calories 257 / Fat 28g / Protein 47g / Carbs 2g / Fiber 1g / Net Carbs 1g

Tex Mex Stir Fry

Serves: 4 / Prep time: 15 minutes / Cook time: 15 minutes

An easy to prepare meal with all the bold flavors from south of the border. The best part is, you can have it on the table in just 30 minutes.

Ingredients:
12 oz. pork tenderloin
4 slices hickory bacon, chopped
1 red bell pepper, cut in strips
1 onion, halved & sliced thin
1 chipotle chili, chopped
2 cloves garlic, chopped
3 cups lettuce, chopped
1 tbsp. olive oil
1 tsp. cumin
1 tsp. oregano

Instructions:
1. Slice tenderloin in half lengthwise, and then cut crosswise thinly. Toss pork, bacon, and chipotle pieces together in a bowl; set aside.
2. Heat oil in a large skillet over medium-high heat. Add bell pepper and onion and cook, stirring often, until almost tender, about 3-4 minutes. Transfer to a bowl.
3. Add pork mixture to the skillet and cook, stirring often, for 3-4 minutes, until bacon is crisp and pork is no longer pink.
5. Return vegetables to the pan and cook until heated through. Serve over a bed of lettuce.

Nutrition Facts Per Serving
Calories 322 / Fat 18g / Protein 34g / Carbs 5g / Fiber 1g / Net Carbs 4g

Turkey Cutlets with Dijon Sauce

Serves: 2 / Prep time: 10 minutes / Cook time: 15 minutes

Don't let the list of ingredients scare you. These delicious turkey cutlets are easy to make and a great way to impress that special someone.

Ingredients:
2 turkey cutlets
1 shallot, sliced thin
1 clove garlic, chopped fine
½ lemon, juiced
½ cup dry white wine
2 tbsp. olive oil, divided
2 tbsp. flour
1 tbsp. fresh rosemary, chopped
1 tbsp. fresh parsley, chopped
½ tbsp. lemon zest
1 tsp. Dijon mustard
½ tsp. salt
¼ tsp. pepper

Instructions
1. Place turkey cutlets between 2 pieces of plastic wrap and pound to ½-inch thick. Place them in a large bowl.
2. In a small bowl, combine parsley, rosemary, garlic, zest, salt, and pepper and mix well.
3. Brush both sides of cutlets with ½ tbsp. of the oil and sprinkle with seasoning mixture. Cover and refrigerate 1 hour or overnight.
4. Place the flour in a shallow dish and dredge both sides of turkey. Let sit 2-3 minutes.
5. Heat remaining oil in a large skillet over medium-high heat. Add cutlets and cook 3-5 minutes per side until nicely browned and cooked through. Transfer to a plate and keep warm.
6. Reduce heat to medium and add the shallot to the skillet. Cook 2-3 minutes until shallot softens. Stir in lemon juice, wine, and mustard and cook 2-3 minutes until sauce reduces slightly.
7. Transfer cutlets to serving plates and top with sauce. Serve immediately.

Nutrition Facts Per Serving
Calories 372 / Fat 23g / Protein 21g / Carbs 10g / Fiber 1g / Net Carbs 9g

Seafood & Fish

Cajun Salmon

Serves: 4 / Prep time: 5 minutes / Cook time: 10 minutes

Blackened salmon with just enough heat to wake up your taste buds. This tasty dish cooks up quickly and is ideal for an easy weeknight dinner.

Ingredients:
4 salmon filets, skin on
1 lemon, cut in wedges
2 tbsp. olive oil
1 tbsp. sweet paprika, plus 1 tsp.
1 tsp. garlic powder
1 tsp. oregano
1 tsp. salt
¾ tsp. cayenne pepper

Instructions
1. In a shallow dish, combine all the seasonings. Press the salmon filets, flesh side down, into the seasonings to coat well.
2. Heat the oil in a large skillet over medium-high heat. Place the salmon, skin side up, in the pan and cook until blackened, about 3 minutes.
3. Turn the filets over and cook another 5-7 minutes, or until they reach desired doneness. Serve immediately with lemon wedges.

Nutrition Facts Per Serving
Calories 313 / Fat 18g / Protein 34g / Carbs 3g / Fiber 1g / Net Carbs 2g

Crab Mac 'N' Cheese

Serves: 4 / Prep time: 10 minutes / Cook time: 40 minutes

Lump crabmeat with plenty of melted cheese and cauliflower—a delicious twist to ordinary mac 'n' cheese. This decadent dish is healthy and sure to please everyone.

Ingredients:
1 egg
3 cups cauliflower, separated into florets
½ cup heavy cream
½ cup cheddar cheese, grated
3 oz. lump crab
1 ½ oz. pork rinds, crushed
2 tbsp. Parmesan cheese
1 tbsp. butter, cut in small pieces
¼ tsp. salt
¼ tsp. pepper

Instructions
1. Preheat oven to 350 degrees.
2. In a large bowl, beat the egg, cream, salt, pepper, and cheddar cheese until combined.
3. Fold in cauliflower and crab and gently mix to combine. Transfer to an 8-inch baking dish.
4. In a separate bowl, combine the pork rinds and Parmesan cheese. Sprinkle over the crab mixture.
5. Top with butter and bake 40 minutes until golden brown and bubbly. Let cool 5 minutes before serving.

Nutrition Facts Per Serving
Calories 254 / Fat 19g / Protein 18g / Carbs 5g / Fiber 3g / Net Carbs 3g

Creamy Clam Chowder

Serves: 6 / Prep time: 10 minutes / Cook time: 3 hours

This easy clam chowder cooks in the crock pot, so no need to heat up your kitchen. Enjoy it anytime of the year when you are craving something comforting.

Ingredients:
5 slices bacon, chopped
2 cloves garlic, chopped fine
1 bay leaf
½ onion, chopped
3 cups cauliflower, separated in florets
1 cup almond milk, unsweetened
1 cup heavy cream
1 cup chicken broth, low-sodium
18 oz. clams, chopped & drained
4 oz. cream cheese
2 tbsp. fresh parsley, chopped
½ tsp. thyme

Instructions
1. Cook the bacon in a skillet over medium-high heat until crisp. Transfer to paper towel-lined plate. Drain all but 3 tbsp. of the fat.
2. Add the onion and garlic and cook 2-3 minutes, until onion is translucent. Add the thyme and cook 1 minute more. Transfer to the crock pot.
3. Stir in the broth, cream cheese, clams, bay leaf, and cauliflower. Mix until combined. Cover with the lid and cook on low heat 2-3 hours until cauliflower is tender. Stir in the milk and cream and cook until heated through.
4. Ladle into bowls and top with bacon and parsley. Serve warm.

Nutrition Facts Per Serving
Calories 377 / Fat 24g / Protein 27g / Carbs 13g / Fiber 1g / Net Carbs 12g

Ginger Lime Glazed Salmon

Serves: 4 / Prep time: 5 minutes / Cook time: 10 minutes

The zesty flavors of lime and ginger come together in this tasty glazed salmon. It is the perfect meal to make on a hot summer day.

Ingredients:
4 salmon fillets
1/3 cup stevia brown sugar, packed
3 tbsp. fish sauce
1 ½ tbsp. soy sauce
1 tbsp. fresh lime juice
1 tbsp. coconut oil, melted
1 tbsp. green onions, sliced
1 tbsp. cilantro, chopped
2 tsp. lime zest, finely grated
1 tsp. fresh ginger, peeled & grated
½ tsp. pepper

Instructions:
1. Add the oil, brown sugar, fish sauce, soy sauce, ginger, zest, juice, and pepper to a large, deep skillet. Stir to mix.
2. Bring to a simmer over medium heat, stirring often. Add the salmon and cover with the sauce. Let cook 5-8 minutes, or until fish flakes easily with a fork and bottom side is caramelized. Transfer to a serving dish with caramelized side up.
3. Continue cooking sauce until it has thickened, about 3-4 minutes. Spoon over fish and garnish with green onions and cilantro. Serve.

Nutrition Facts Per Serving
Calories 316 / Fat 18g / Protein 35g / Carbs 5g / Fiber 0g / Net Carbs 5g

Parmesan Cod Nuggets

Serves: 4 / Prep time: 10 minutes / Cook time: 10 minutes

Crispy fish nuggets flavored with Parmesan cheese make a great lunch or quick dinner. These fish nuggets are also gluten-free.

Ingredients:
2 eggs
1 lb. cod, cut into bite-sized nuggets
1 ½ cups Parmesan cheese
1 cup almond flour
3 tbsp. olive oil
¼ tsp. salt
¼ tsp. pepper

Instructions
1. Pat cod dry with paper towels.
2. In a medium bowl, beat the eggs.
3. In a separate bowl, sift the flour.
4. In a third bowl, combine Parmesan cheese, salt, and pepper.
5. Heat oil in a large skillet over medium-high heat.
6. Dip each piece of cod first in flour, then egg, and finally in Parmesan mixture. Place the fish in the skillet, don't overcrowd them.
7. Cook 8-10 minutes, flipping them halfway through, until golden brown. Repeat with any remaining cod.

Nutrition Facts Per Serving
Calories 363 / Fat 20g / Protein 34g / Carbs 6g / Fiber 3g / Net Carbs 3g

Salmon & Spinach Skillet

Serves: 4 / Prep time: 5 minutes / Cook time: 15 minutes

A tasty meal that is table ready in less than 30 minutes. This one-pan dinner is packed with vitamins and nutrients and so tasty you will want to make it again and again.

Ingredients:
4 salmon filets
4 cloves garlic, chopped fine
10 oz. fresh spinach
2 tbsp. olive oil, divided
½ tbsp. lemon juice
½ tsp. salt
¼ tsp. pepper
¼ tsp. basil

Instructions
1. Heat 1 tbsp. oil in a large skillet on medium heat.
2. Season salmon with salt and pepper and add to the pan. Cook 8-10 minutes, or until fish flakes easily with a fork, turning over halfway through cooking time. Transfer to a plate.
3. Add remaining oil and let heat up. Add remaining ingredients and cook 2-3 minutes, until spinach is wilted.
4. Place fish on serving plates and top with spinach mixture. Serve immediately.

Nutrition Facts Per Serving
Calories 436 / Fat 30g / Protein 37g / Carbs 4g / Fiber 2g / Net Carbs 2g

Shrimp Scampi

Serves: 4 / Prep time: 5 minutes / Cook time: 10 minutes

Butter, garlic, and fresh herbs combine to make this shrimp dish pop. Serve over our keto-friendly noodles or with cauliflower rice for a complete meal.

Ingredients:
1 lb. shrimp, peeled & deveined
4 tbsp. butter
2 tbsp. white wine
1 tbsp. garlic, diced fine
1 tbsp. lemon juice
1 tbsp. fresh chives, chopped
1 tbsp. fresh basil, chopped fine
2 tsp. crushed red pepper

Instructions
1. Melt butter in a large skillet over medium heat. Add garlic and red pepper flakes and cook, stirring, 1 minute.
2. Add remaining ingredients and stir gently to coat the shrimp. Cook, stirring often, until shrimp turn pink. Let sit 1 minute before serving.

Nutrition Facts Per Serving
Calories 250 / Fat 14g / Protein 26g / Carbs 3g / Fiber 0g / Net Carbs 3g

Steamed Spanish Clams

Serves: 6 / Prep time: 5 minutes / Cook time: 20 minutes

These steamed clams are full of bold flavors. They are quick and easy to prepare and sure to impress your guests.

Ingredients:
36 littleneck clams
1 onion, chopped fine
¼ cup dry sherry
3 oz. prosciutto, chopped
3 tbsp. olive oil

Instructions
1. Heat the oil in a large pot over medium-high heat. Add the onion and cook 1 minute. Cover, reduce heat to low, and cook 10-15 minutes, until onion is soft.
3. Stir in remaining ingredients and increase heat to medium. Cover and cook 5 minutes, or until the clams open.
4. Discard any unopened clams and serve immediately.

Nutrition Facts Per Serving
Calories 166 / Fat 9g / Protein 15g / Carbs 5g / Fiber 1g / Net Carbs 4g

Veggies & Sides

Bacon & Goat Cheese Brussel Sprouts

Serves: 6 / Prep time: 10 minutes / Cook time: 15 minutes

A tasty side dish combining Brussel sprouts, soft goat cheese, and bacon—the perfect complement to almost any meat entrée.

Ingredients:
1 lb. Brussels sprouts, trimmed & cut in half
3 slices bacon, chopped
2 cloves garlic, diced fine
¼ cup water
3 oz. goat cheese, soft
2 tbsp. milk
1 tbsp. Parmesan cheese
2 tsp. olive oil
1 tsp. paprika
¼ tsp. salt
¼ tsp. pepper

Instructions
1. Cook bacon in a large skillet over medium-high heat until crisp. Transfer to paper towel-lined plate.
2. Add oil to the pan and let it get hot. Add Brussel sprouts and cook, stirring frequently, 5 minutes, or until they start to brown.
3. Add water, cover and cook another 5 minutes, or until fork-tender. Drain any water from the pot.
4. Stir in goat cheese, milk, Parmesan, salt, and pepper. Cook, stirring frequently, until cheese has melted.
5. Stir in bacon and cook until heated through. Sprinkle with paprika and serve.

Nutrition Facts Per Serving
Calories 106 / Fat 6g / Protein 7g / Carbs 8g / Fiber 3g / Net Carbs 5g

Basic Cauliflower Rice

Serves: 4 / Prep time: 5 minutes / Cook time: 10 minutes

Use this basic recipe as a substitute for white rice in any recipe. It works great for dishes that are served with sauce. Or, get creative and add your favorite cheese and veggies and create a side dish of your own.

Ingredients:
1 small head of cauliflower, grated
1 clove of garlic, diced fine
1 tbsp. olive oil
½ tsp. salt

Instructions
1. Heat oil in a large skillet over medium-high heat. Add the garlic and cook 1 minute, stirring often.
2. Stir in cauliflower and cook until tender, about 7-9 minutes, stirring occasionally. Serve.

Nutrition Facts Per Serving
Calories 48 / Fat 4g / Protein 1g / Carbs 4g / Fiber 2g / Net Carbs 2g

Cheesy Cauliflower Mash

Serves: 6 / Prep time: 5 minutes / Cook time: 15 minutes

This tasty, cheesy mashed cauliflower is a healthier alternative to mashed potatoes. Now you can enjoy all the flavor without all the calories and carbs. So good, even the kids will love it.

Ingredients:
2 ½ lbs. cauliflower florets, steamed
4 oz. sharp cheddar cheese, grated
2 tbsp. half-and-half
1 tbsp. butter
½ tsp. salt
½ tsp. pepper

Instructions
1. Steam the cauliflower until it is fork-tender, drain well.
2. Add the cauliflower, along with the remaining ingredients, to a food processor. Pulse until almost smooth. Serve warm.
3. If preferred, you can make it ahead of time and just reheat it as needed.

Nutrition Facts Per Serving
Calories 145 / Fat 9g / Protein 9g / Carbs 10g / Fiber 5g / Net Carbs 5g

Creamy Baked Squash

Serves: 6 / Prep time: 10 minutes / Cook time: 40 minutes

This casserole is a great way to use summer squash. Mixed with creamy mayonnaise and melted cheese, the kids may even like it.

Ingredients:
2 eggs
2 lbs. summer squash, cut in 1-inch pieces
¾ cup sharp cheddar cheese, reduced fat, grated & divided
¼ cup mayonnaise
¼ tsp. salt
¼ tsp. pepper

Instructions
1. Preheat oven to 375 degrees. Spray a 2-quart baking dish with cooking spray.
2. Place the squash in a large pot with just enough water to cover it. Bring to a boil over medium-high heat. Once boiling, reduce heat to medium and cook until tender, about 8-10 minutes. Drain.
3. Place the squash in a large bowl and add ½ cup cheese, mayonnaise, eggs, salt, and pepper and mix well. Spoon into prepared dish and sprinkle with remaining cheese.
4. Bake 30 minutes, until top is golden brown and casserole is heated through. Serve.

Nutrition Facts Per Serving
Calories 120 / Fat 8g / Protein 7g / Carbs 6g / Fiber 2g / Net Carbs 4g

Fried Green Beans

Serves: 8 / Prep time: 5 minutes / Cook time: 10 minutes

These crispy fried green beans are a great alternative to fries or the same ol' cauliflower tots. And since they don't use any bread crumbs or flour, they are gluten-free too.

Ingredients:
1 egg
12 oz. fresh green beans, trimmed
¾ cup pork rinds, crushed
¼ cup parmesan cheese
¼ cup olive oil
1 tbsp. water
1 tsp. garlic powder
¼ tsp. salt
1/8 tsp. cayenne pepper

Instructions
1. Heat oil in a large saucepan over medium-high heat.
2. In a shallow dish, stir together pork rinds, parmesan, garlic powder, salt, and pepper.
3. In a separate shallow dish, whisk together egg and water.
4. Dip beans first in egg, then in crumb mixture.
5. Cook the beans (in batches) in the hot oil until golden brown and crisp. Transfer to paper towel-lined plate. Serve immediately.

Nutrition Facts Per Serving
Calories 197 / Fat 11g / Protein 20g / Carbs 3g / Fiber 2g / Net Carbs 1g

Asparagus and Salmon

Serves: 2 / Prep time: 10 minutes / Cook time: 15 minutes

If you are looking for a delicious seafood dish, then don't look any further! I mean, what could be better than preparing the King of all Fish, the salmon with some healthy asparagus? The cheese and butter just kicks up the "Keto" factor of this dish further while making it even more delicious.

Ingredients:
2 salmon fillets, 6 ounces each, skin on
Salt to taste
1 pound asparagus, trimmed
2 garlic cloves, minced
3 tablespoons butter
¼ cup parmesan cheese, grated

Instructions
1. Preheat your oven to 400 degrees F
2. Take a baking sheet and grease it with oil
3. Take your kitchen towel and pat Salmon dry, season well with salt
4. Transfer salmon to your baking dish and arrange the asparagus around it
5. Take a pan and place it over medium heat, add butter and let the butter melt
6. Add garlic and cook for 3 minutes until slightly brown
7. Drizzle the garlic butter sauce over salmon
8. Bake for 12 minutes until Salmon is flaky
9. Serve and enjoy!

Nutrition Facts Per Serving
Calories: 434 / Fat: 26g / Protein: 42g / Carbohydrates: 6g / Fiber: 2g / Net Carbs: 4g

Mushroom & Spinach Cauliflower Rice

Serves: 4 / Prep time: 10 minutes / Cook time: 15 minutes

A tasty side dish that pairs well with almost any meat entrée. Grated cauliflower is the perfect substitute for rice in any recipe since it has the same texture once cooked, without the same amount of carbs and calories.

Ingredients:
2 cloves garlic, chopped fine
3 cups mushrooms, sliced
2 cups cauliflower, grated
2 cups spinach
½ cup onion, chopped
1 tbsp. olive oil
1 tbsp. soy sauce

Instructions
1. Heat oil in a large skillet on medium heat. Add the cauliflower and onion and cook 3-5 minutes, stirring frequently, until onion is soft.
2. Stir in mushrooms and cook until tender, and most of the liquid has been absorbed, about 3-5 minutes. Stir in the garlic and cook 1 minute more.
3. Stir in the soy sauce and cook about 1 minute, until it is absorbed by the cauliflower. Add the spinach and cook until wilted, about 2 minutes. Serve immediately.

Nutrition Facts Per Serving
Calories 58 / Fat 4g / Protein 2g / Carbs 5g / Fiber 2g / Net Carbs 3g

Roasted Italian Broccoli

Serves: 2 / Prep time: 5 minutes / Cook time: 15 minutes

Broccoli flavored with Italian seasonings that is roasted until crispy is a tasty side dish to any meal. Since the topping uses crushed pork rinds, this recipe is gluten-free too.

Ingredients:
2 cups broccoli florets
2 tbsp. pork rinds, crushed
1 tbsp. olive oil
2 tsp. Italian seasoning

Instructions
1. Preheat oven to 300 degrees.
2. In a large bowl, combine all ingredients and toss well. Spread on a large baking sheet.
3. Bake 10-15 minutes, until broccoli is tender on the inside, stirring halfway through cooking time. Serve immediately.

Nutrition Facts Per Serving
Calories 176 / Fat 12g / Protein 12g / Carbs 7g / Fiber 2g / Net Carbs 5g

References

Masood W, Uppaluri KR. Ketogenic Diet. [Updated 2019 Mar 21]. In: StatPearls [Internet]. Treasure Island (FL): StatPearls Publishing; 2019 Jan-. Available from: https://www.ncbi.nlm.nih.gov/books/NBK499830/

Bonjour JP. Dietary protein: an essential nutrient for bone health. J Am Coll Nutr. 2005;24(6 Suppl):526S-36S.

Shams-white MM, Chung M, Du M, et al. Dietary protein and bone health: a systematic review and meta-analysis from the National Osteoporosis Foundation. Am J Clin Nutr. 2017;105(6):1528-1543.

Koopman R, Beelen M, Stellingwerff T, et al. Coingestion of carbohydrate with protein does not further augment postexercise muscle protein synthesis. Am J Physiol Endocrinol Metab. 2007;293(3):E833-42.

Zuñiga YL, Rebello SA, Oi PL, et al. Rice and noodle consumption is associated with insulin resistance and hyperglycemia in an Asian population. Br J Nutr. 2014;111(6):1118-28.

Jung CH, Choi KM. Impact of High-Carbohydrate Diet on Metabolic Parameters in Patients with Type 2 Diabetes. Nutrients. 2017;9(4)

"Dietary Fats." Heart.org, American Heart Association, 23 Mar. 2014, www.heart.org/en/healthy-living/healthy-eating/eat-smart/fats/dietary-fats.

Gomes, Júnia Maria Geraldo, Fabrini, Sabrina Pinheiro, & Alfenas, Rita de Cássia Gonçalves. (2017). Low glycemic index diet reduces body fat and attenuates inflammatory and metabolic responses in patients with type 2 diabetes. Archives of Endocrinology and Metabolism, 61(2), 137-144. Epub September 05, 2016.https://dx.doi.org/10.1590/2359-3997000000206

Shenkin, A. "Micronutrients in health and disease." Postgraduate medical journal vol. 82,971 (2006): 559-67. doi:10.1136/pgmj.2006.047670

Belinda Lennerz, Jochen K Lennerz, Food Addiction, High-Glycemic-Index Carbohydrates, and Obesity, Clinical Chemistry, Volume 64, Issue 1, 1 January 2018, Pages 64–71

O'donnell M, Mente A, Rangarajan S, et al. Urinary sodium and potassium excretion, mortality, and cardiovascular events. N Engl J Med. 2014;371(7):612-23.

Cao JJ, Nielsen FH. Acid diet (high-meat protein) effects on calcium metabolism and bone health. Curr Opin Clin Nutr Metab Care. 2010;13(6):698-702.

Daley, Cynthia A et al. "A review of fatty acid profiles and antioxidant content in grass-fed and grain-fed beef." Nutrition journal vol. 9 10. 10 Mar. 2010, doi:10.1186/1475-2891-9-10

Lam, Yan Y, and Eric Ravussin. "Analysis of energy metabolism in humans: A review of methodologies." Molecular metabolism vol. 5,11 1057-1071. 20 Sep. 2016, doi:10.1016/j.molmet.2016.09.005

Rebolledo, Julio A, and Regina Arellano. "Cultural Differences and Considerations When Initiating Insulin." Diabetes spectrum : a publication of the American Diabetes Association vol. 29,3 (2016): 185-90. doi:10.2337/diaspect.29.3.185

Khatri, M. (2019, November 6). Type 2 Diabetes: Symptoms, Causes, Diagnosis, and Treatment. Retrieved from https://www.webmd.com/diabetes/type-2-diabetes#1

Adapted from U.S. Department of Health and Human Services. 2008 Physical Activity Guidelines for Americans. Washington (DC): U.S. Department of Health and Human Services; 2008. Available at: http://www.health.gov/paguidelines. Accessed August 6, 2015.

Soleimani, Manoocher Insulin resistance and hypertension: new insights

Kidney International, Volume 87, Issue 3, 497 - 499

Weber DD, Aminazdeh-gohari S, Kofler B. Ketogenic diet in cancer therapy. Aging (Albany NY). 2018;10(2):164-165.

De groot S, Pijl H, Van der hoeven JJM, Kroep JR. Effects of short-term fasting on cancer treatment. J Exp Clin Cancer Res. 2019;38(1):209.

Wu G. Dietary protein intake and human health. Food & function. 2016; 7(3):1251-65.

Feinman, R. D. (2015, January). Dietary carbohydrate restriction: Compelling theory for further research. https://www.sciencedirect.com/science/article/abs/pii/S089990071500115X

www.ingramcontent.com/pod-product-compliance
Lightning Source LLC
Chambersburg PA
CBHW080025130526
44591CB00037B/2675